CONQUERING
EVIL *with the* POWER
of the CROSS

CaN
CORRUPTION
be defeated?

CONQUERING

EVIL *with the* POWER

of the CROSS

CaN CORRUPTION be defeated?

ANGELITA MARASIGAN

CREATION HOUSE

CAN CORRUPTION BE DEFEATED? by Angelita Marasigan
Published by Creation House
A Charisma Media Company
600 Rinehart Road
Lake Mary, Florida 32746
www.charismamedia.com

Unless otherwise marked, Scripture quotations are from the New King James Version of the Bible. Copyright © 1979, 1980, 1982 by Thomas Nelson, Inc., publishers. Used by permission

Scripture quotations marked AMP are from the Amplified Bible. Old Testament copyright © 1965, 1987 by the Zondervan Corporation. The Amplified New Testament copyright © 1954, 1958, 1987 by the Lockman Foundation. Used by permission.

Design Director: Bill Johnson
Cover design by Rachel Lopez

Visit the author by e-mail: drealissue@rogers.com

Library of Congress Cataloging-in-Publication Data: 2011923395
International Standard Book Number: 978-1-61638-481-4

12 13 14 15 — 9 8 7 6 5 4 3 2
Printed in the United States of America

Dedication

*To all those who have taken the righteous
cause of the fight against corruption that
impoverish peoples in the world: may they
overcome in the righteousness of God.*

*To all my grandchildren, and their generation
and those after them, that they may realize
the causes of corruption and have the
grace to avoid and overcome its evil.*

*To all those whom the Lord had used in one way
or another for this book to become a reality: the
Lord heard your prayers; God saw the labors of
your love; He will bless you beyond measure.*

*To all the readers of this book: that they may
understand the real issue behind corruption
and that they may gain wisdom.*

ACKNOWLEDGMENT

To God, my heavenly Father and Savior Jesus Christ: in whom, through whom, and for whom this book came into being. And, to the Holy Spirit: who taught me and led me through all the years; teaching me the truths of His will in my life, in this world.

TABLE OF CONTENTS

INTRODUCTION

I TOOK UP ENGINEERING studies after high school, not because of the money I would earn as an engineer but because of my love for math, even though I was not good at it. One of the requirements during my studies was a course in engineering contracts and specifications, which included ethics. This course did not involve math, and I did not like it at the time. But it was part of my required studies, so I had to take it.

Little did I know that the Lord's hand, even then, was preparing me for the work assignment I would receive later. In this job, ethics were involved in the bulk of my work as an engineer. In my work on project development and contracts administration, I was involved with design, project estimates, writing tender documents, bidder prequalification documents, project specifications, and contract documents. These are requirements, guidelines, and conditions concerning the projects tendered, the conditions for tendering, and the evaluation of bids. I must select bidders based on their qualifications, call and accept tenders, recommend awards, and prepare contract agreements.

Needless to say, I encounter ethics issues every day. In

fact, I encounter quite a bit of corrupting influences as well. And way back in the beginning of my studies, God made sure I learned the basic things I would need for this future job. It amazes me to know God ordered my life and prepared me with what I would need in advance. He wrote down everything, the days fashioned for me, and what I would do when as yet there were none of them (Ps. 139:16).

I love my job, as I walk through a project from its conception stage to its development stage and then see it completed and ready to be used with my own eyes. The job is challenging, as it requires me to foresee and prevent potential problems, conflicts, and discourage corruption. I have to try my best to plug any loopholes or gray areas in the process that might be compromised by wrong motives of unscrupulous persons.

During the course of doing this job for many years, the Lord made me observe people who struggled to decide between right and wrong choices in the midst of a work culture that was prone to corruption. In the chapters of this book, I share the lessons I have learned from this job through observing these things in a work environment.

I was burdened to write this book because of the many news reports I hear and read about corruption. Corruption scandals occur in the public and the private sector every day. Many say that global poverty, which keeps getting worse and worse, is directly related to and caused by corruption.

God's plan was for man to be blessed and prosperous. He didn't plan poverty for man. However, God's plan for the good of man was hindered in Adam's fall. Poverty now exists, and it has existed throughout human history, just as Jesus said: "For you have the poor with you always" (Matt. 26:11).

Even in this modern age, the number of poor people around the world continues to increase as the level of their poverty continues to decrease. Despite the improvements and progress in the world, this continues. Why? Could something be causing it? I contend that poverty and suffering in this world is directly caused by corruption, and we'll explore who could be powering corruption as it afflicts governments, businesses, institutions, and mankind.

This book deals with the choices we face and the decisions we make in the workplace, in the marketplace, at home, and in all of life where we meet corruptive influences. The workplace, the marketplace, and the home are places where money, prestige, and prosperity are used to measure success. These are the favorite places for "mammon," or the love of money, to establish its rule, thereby opening an entry point for corruption to gain influence. In these places, you often have to choose between right, wrong, or being complacent and doing nothing at all (which is almost the same thing as choosing wrong).

Corruption is a monster you have to fight to set free the

multitudes of poor people around the world and to alleviate them from their suffering. Lately, people in many nations are rising up and demonstrating in the streets with a common cry against their leaders. Powers are shaking. Governments are crumbling. People are rising up against corruption.

Join me in the fight against corruption in the pages of this book—and in the way you live your life from this point on.

Chapter 1

LIFE'S
TWO CHOICES

O NE OF THE most dangerous situations a swimmer ever encounters is getting caught in a rip current. A rip current is a narrow, fast-moving section of water in a sea or lake that forms from the impact of wind-generated waves and travels in a direction away from shore to deeper water instead of dissipating parallel to the shoreline like most waves do. Rip current speeds can reach as high as eight feet per second—faster than Olympic swimmers can swim—making them dangerous to swimmers and non-swimmers alike. The force and speed of a rip current can sweep even a very strong swimmer out to sea.[1]

The best way to escape a rip current is to swim parallel

to the shoreline, away from the current instead of toward it. Or the swimmer can try to stay afloat and let himself be carried out to sea. Sometimes the current can push a swimmer hundreds of yards away from shore, so this can be quite dangerous.

It is important for a person caught in this situation to think clearly, not to panic, and to keep his head above water so he can breathe. The important thing is for him to never to exhaust himself fighting the current because its force is very strong.[2]

When caught in a rip current, a person may try swimming back to shore to protect himself but not realize he is swimming against the force of a current as it heads back out to sea. This person might have great trust in himself, but his efforts are no match against this force. Others, with determination and strength, will skirt and maneuver their way out of the rip current to avoid drowning. Still others will be overtaken by fear and choose to do nothing, thus being swept off with the rip current farther from the beach. These individuals are just waiting for whatever will happen, to happen.

What if you find yourself far from the shore, in the middle of a lake or sea where the water is very deep, where you have no other choice but to swim or try to stay afloat to keep yourself alive? The problem concerns your survival. What will you do? Will you back off? Will you allow fear to immobilize your thoughts? Will you submit yourself to fear? Will you do nothing to avoid the force of the current? Will you use all the strategies you can think of to steer yourself safely to your destination? Will you maneuver your way out to escape the pressure of the rip current? This last option may sound risky but is actually the right thing to do.

You have only two choices before you: maneuver around the riptide or do nothing. But you have to make the choice immediately because the situation is fluid. It is moving. Risky. Powerful. It carries a destructive force. You cannot say, "Wait." You have to make the right decision right away to prevent grave consequences. The wrong choice or no choice at all makes the consequences worse.

Situations like these occur in your everyday life, and especially in your job. You are always confronted with the choice between two or more options: the right or the wrong choice; good or evil; blessing or curse; life or death. No one can live with two choices at the same time, for they will either be blessed for choosing the right one or sorry for choosing the wrong one. (See Luke 16:13.) There is no middle ground here. Sometimes the choice is not so difficult because it is between the better and the best choice, but there is always the option not to make any choice at all. The Bible admonished, "Do your best in whatever you have to do as doing it for God and not for man" (Eph. 6:6–7, author's paraphrase).

When you make no choice at all or do nothing, the bad

option prevails, for even if you know the good that you ought to do and do not do it, you are doing wrong; it is sin (James 4:17). We always have to choose the right choices in order to have a good life and to prosper—and the good choice is to love God, obey His voice, and hold on tight to Him (Deut. 30:20). If you do these things, God will order your life right before Him and before men, and He will prosper you.

If you love God, then you will fear doing wrong (Prov. 8:13). The loving fear of God will lead you to choose that which is morally right, even if doing the right thing makes you appear foolish in the eyes of those around you who think otherwise. This is when you will feel the pressure and intimidation coming against you. Unless you have wisdom and great strength to stand on your moral convictions, you will be influenced by the wrong choices of other people around you.

It is important to become aware of the place you are and the people you are with. It is important to know if you are in an environment where it is a common practice—a culture—to accept what is morally wrong as normal. You may discover you are in a corrupt place with people influenced by the world. This is a difficult place to be if you love God and hate what is wrong. (See Psalm 97:10.)

What will you do? Will you insist on doing that which you believe in your conscience is the right thing to do?

Will you be willing to receive the ridicule, the rejection, and the intimidation of those who follow the flow?

The first choice—that of swimming around the current, refusing to go with the flow—is really the right choice, but it is a difficult choice to make in that kind of environment, and you need a lot of strength to stand firmly on your moral convictions. The second choice gives you the option to go with the norms of the world. Closing your eyes to what is happening around you seems like the safest thing to do—but in doing so, you essentially allow the wrong practices and the wrong principles to get firmly entrenched in you and your environment. You indirectly participate in the wrong thing that is happening around you.

The Bible says, "Do not be conformed to this world, but be transformed by the renewing of your mind, that you may prove what is that good and acceptable and perfect will of God" (Rom. 12:2). The Lord searches the heart and tests the mind of man, and it is God who will work in you, *if you submit to Him*, both to will and to do for His good pleasure. (See Jeremiah 17:10 and Philippians 2:13.) Jesus said, "Take heed that no one deceives you" (Matt. 24:4).

In this book, you will learn how to live this way.

Chapter 2

SEATED ON
MY FATHER'S LAP

M Y FATHER IS a godly man. I often heard my mother tell the story of my father spending the first hour of the New Year praying on his knees inside his room. Another memory of him from my childhood is etched in my mind—that of sitting on my father's lap some moonlit evenings, feeling so snug and safe. I enjoyed the company of my father and my mother as they talked to each other on those nights. Their favorite place to sit was near the window, facing a nearby field. I would look outside the window and see small dwarf-like creatures with pointed hats walking back and forth in the field in the moonlight. I thought those creatures were there during the nighttime the same way people worked there during the day. I felt no fear. I felt comfortably safe seated on my father's lap.

As I reminisce about this memory, the apostle Paul's words to the church in Ephesus comes to mind: "At one time you walked [habitually]. You were following the course and fashion of this world [were under the sway of the tendency of this present age], following the prince of the power of the air. [You were obedient to and under the control of] the [demon] spirit that still constantly works in the sons of disobedience [the careless, the rebellious, and the unbelieving, who go against the purposes of God]" (Eph. 2:2, AMP).

Now I understand the vision I had of the dwarf-like creatures walking back and forth in the field. They were demon spirits, seeking people to be snatched and placed under the control of Satan. They were active in the night, when it was dark, because that's when they like to work best.

When you are in a situation where everything seems messed up, dark, and hopeless, then, it is very likely that demons under the direction of Satan are actively walking about, lurking in your midst. They are looking for an opportune moment to entice and attack so they can take control of your life.

Once you give in to their temptations and desire is conceived in your heart, sin is birthed into your life. Once sin is birthed, corruption starts its process in your life. And corruption, being a rotten process, ultimately leads to death (James 1:14–15). Those who don't know how to do right and instead do corrupt things are pursued by an adversary who will sap their strength and plunder their lives (Amos 3:10–11).

At this point of decision, you are in a situation like the one we read about in chapter one. You are being asked to choose between right and wrong. Here you must remember: "There is a way that seems right for a man, but its end is the way of death," for "every way of a man is right in his own eyes, but the LORD weighs the hearts" (Prov. 14:12; 21:2). You face two major choices, but you have only one choice to make. You cannot choose two options at the same time, for you will be happy with one and sorry with the other or else hate the one and love the other, for "you cannot serve God and mammon" (Luke 16:13).

Human choices based on worldly wisdom and observation often lead to wrong results. Once a wrong choice is chosen, the consequences follow. The principle of planting and reaping always works:

> Do not be deceived, God is not mocked; for whatever a man sows, that he will also reap. For he who sows to [the desires of] his flesh will of the flesh reap corruption, but he who sows to the Spirit will of the Spirit reap everlasting life.
>
> —GALATIANS 6:6–7

Also:

> If you say, "Surely we did not know this," does
> not He who weighs the hearts consider it? He
> who keeps your soul, does He not know it?
> And will He not render to each man according
> to his deeds?
>
> —PROVERBS 24:12

If you "sow the wind" you will "reap the whirlwind"
(Hos. 8:7). The consequences of a wrong choice cannot be
reversed. He who sows iniquity will reap corruption.

But if your choice is based on godly wisdom, you will
be blessed:

> For he who sows to his flesh will of the flesh
> reap corruption but he who sows to the Spirit
> will of the Spirit reap everlasting life.
>
> —GALATIANS 6:8

Also:

> The fear of the LORD is the beginning of
> wisdom, and the knowledge of the Holy One
> is understanding.
>
> —PROVERBS 9:10

You may think your ways are right, but the Lord sees
and knows your heart (Prov. 21:2). If you do what is right
and good in the sight of the Lord, it will be well with you

and you will enter into His blessing and promises (Deut. 6:18). God has set before you life and corruption, blessing and cursing (Deut. 30:19). If you are wise, you will understand and do the things that are good. If you are cautious, you will do what is right before God and not follow the ways of others who walk blindly in the way of corruption.

The ways of the Lord are right. Those who fear God and fear to do evil walk in it, but those with corrupt hearts stumble in them (Hos. 14:9). Therefore, seek God because "those who seek [Him] diligently will find [Him]" (Prov. 8:17), and He will lead those in the right way.

My father's lap was a place of safety, assurance, and comfort, and sitting on his lap took away my fear of the dwarf creatures. I knew my father would take care of me and protect me because he loved me. I was his child, and I felt close to him and very safe on his lap because I completely trusted him.

God is also like a father to those who love Him with reverence and fear: "As a father pities his children, so the LORD pities those who fear Him. For He knows our frame; He remembers that we are dust" (Ps. 103:13–14). If you entrust yourself to the Lord, you will be safe. He will show you His love by taking care of you and protecting you from the enemy, Satan.

God speaks to you as His child: "Come out from among them, the corrupt, and be separate. Do not be like them nor do their ways, and I will receive you. I will be a

Father to you, and you shall be My children" (2 Cor. 6:17–18, author's paraphrase).

Can you trust God? The answer is yes, and without a shadow of a doubt. God is not like a man who lies. What He says He will do, He will do (Num. 23:19). The word that goes forth from God's mouth shall not return void, but it shall accomplish what He pleases, and He prospers it in the thing for which He sent it for (Isa. 55:11). None of God's "words will be postponed any more, but the word which [He speaks] will be done" (Ezek. 12:28). All things shall pass away, but God's words shall remain forever (1 Pet. 1:25). We can trust God, our Father, because He is "the confidence of all the ends of the earth, and of the far-off seas" (Ps. 65:5).

In your life on this earth, you can find safety and assurance for your good when you are seated and abiding in the Father's will. There is no other place of safety except the "rock that is higher" than us, the Lord Jesus (Ps. 61:2). The Bible says, "There is no other name under heaven given among men by which [you] must be saved," other than the name of Jesus (Acts 4:12). At the mention of the name of Jesus, "every knee should bow, of those in heaven, and of those on the earth, and of those under the earth" (Phil. 2:10).

Who can be against us if we are in Jesus? He is "the Alpha and the Omega, the Beginning and the End...who is and who was and who is to come, the Almighty" (Rev. 1:8). You may have tribulations. You may have all kinds of problems that take the breath out of you, but if you have Jesus, you are safe and victorious.

> You may be hard-pressed on every side, yet not crushed; you may be perplexed, but not in despair; persecuted, but not forsaken; struck down, but not destroyed—if you carry about in your body the dying of the Lord Jesus, that the life of Jesus also may be manifested in your body.
>
> —2 Corinthians 4:8–10,
> author's paraphrase

God's plan for man was for his good. After creating Adam and Eve, God blessed them and gave Adam dominion over the earth and everything on it. He also gave them everything they needed to live. The Lord God placed them in the garden eastward in Eden to take care of it, and He commanded Adam to freely eat of the trees growing in the garden except the tree of the knowledge of good and evil, lest on the day he ate of its fruit he would surely die.

God appointed Adam as CEO of all the earth and everything in it. But the idyllic life of Adam in the garden was interrupted and broken by the entrance of corruption, imputed by Satan upon Adam's godly nature because of his disobedience to God's command. The earth also suffered the same corruption process.

But a day is coming when this corruption will be turned into incorruption by the power of Almighty God because what God has planned will come to pass:

> For the earnest expectation of the creation eagerly waits for the revealing of the sons of God. For the creation was subjected to futility, not willingly, but because of Him who subjected it in hope; because the creation itself also will be delivered from the bondage of corruption into the glorious liberty of the children of God.
>
> —ROMANS 8:19–21

Chapter 3

WHAT IS CORRUPTION?

THE WORD *CORRUPTION* is familiar to many. Young and old, rich and poor know this word because it is reported often in the news. The poor blame corruption for their suffering and poverty. Others hate the word and abhor all it represents: the moral and social decadence of a nation. We get frustrated and enraged when we see the harmful things corruption breeds and how it impacts lives around the world. Corruption is a reproach to any people (Prov. 14:34).

Most corruption that is easily noticed and reported is that which occurs in the government or public sector. When corruption occurs, the governed lose their respect and trust in their leaders and the inner workings of their government. With this loss of confidence and respect for leaders, spiritual and moral decline follows. Disobedience to rules of the law and disregard for authority leads to the breakdown of peace and order and the increase of social problems and lawlessness.

The economic cost of corruption in the public sector, although directly absorbed by the government, is eventually passed on to society. Social classes are configured, and the lowest strata—the poor—are pushed down to a rat-like level of existence in some of the most corrupt nations.

Corruption is a curse for a nation and its people. As a social and spiritual sickness and curse, it permeates an entire nation. It curses a nation socially and spiritually.

But what is corruption, really? And why does the mention of corruption—and its byproduct, poverty—influence millions of voters to elect perceived non-corrupt leaders to power? Could it be that the impact and effect of corruption—poverty—has permeated every level of society? Are people fed up with the effects of corruption in their lives? Are they looking for hope of deliverance from this social malady?

People are mad at the corruption that causes them, their families, and the generations that follow to lose their hope of deliverance from the bondage of poverty. They are tired. They are hopeless. They want to be set free from poverty—and most people perceive poverty to be the end result of the social cancer of corruption.

Merriam-Webster's Dictionary defines corruption as "an

impairment of integrity, virtue, or moral principle." It adds further to that definition, "the process of rotting." In short, we learn that corruption means being in a rotten state or being in the process of being turned into a rotten state.

BusinessDictionary.com defines corruption as "giving or obtaining advantage through means which are illegitimate, immoral, and/or inconsistent with one's duty or the rights of others." The INTERPOL Group of Experts on Corruption (IGEC) defines corruption as "any course of action or failure to act by individuals or organizations, public or private, in violation of law or trust for profit or gain."[1]

From the above definitions, we can safely say that corruption is induced by someone with power taking advantage of that power and using it to cause the turning of a person, system, or a thing into a rotten state through illegitimate or immoral ways inconsistent or against their legal duty or the rights of others. Corruption, then, is an immoral state ruled by the spirits of deceit, lying, covetousness, greed, lust, discontentment, a controlling spirit, selfishness, pride, envy, and the love of money.

Just as cancer manifests itself in many forms and attacks different parts of a human body, so does corruption. Corruption can manifest itself in many ways and in many sectors of human society. And just as cancer attacks the body, so can corruption plant itself on people—the unbelieving and the godly.

Corruption can introduce itself anywhere it chooses to

operate, but its favorite operating grounds are the public sector, the private sector, and the marketplace. Once it succeeds in planting itself, corruption grows overwhelmingly fast and shifts into different forms in order to continue clinging tightly to the corrupted people and system. Its impact is devastating, exponential, and life threatening. It grows quietly, hardly noticed, until its evil effects on government, society, and people's lives cannot be hidden anymore because the evidence of decay can be seen and felt.

Here is another way corruption is similar to cancer. Cancer has no known cure. Many are trying to fight it—doctors advise preventative measures to preclude its onset, and palliative measures are used in the management of those in its advanced stages—and these are good intervention measures. But they're never a total cure. These measures are used to prolong the life of one patient at a time, but they don't eliminate the disease of cancer itself.

So it is with corruption and our fight against it. We can adapt our fight against corruption to specific corrupted sectors, but we can only fight them one at a time because corruption works in many ways. It keeps reinventing itself to adapt to different people groups, circumstances, and seasons. Therefore, we must understand corruption beyond its perceived meaning in order to fight it more broadly.

Corruption is big business. It works within a multinational and multiracial network of operations, and its CEO, Satan, is the head of "principalities, powers, rulers of the darkness of this age, and the spiritual hosts of wickedness in the heavenly places" (Eph. 6:12)—in other words, his demons. The main agenda of this Corruptor is to corrupt people, enslave them to poverty, and install lawlessness and hopelessness as a means to corrupt and establish wickedness in the whole world.

The ultimate cost of corruption is massive, and its impact on the world's poor has reached staggering proportions. Of course, respect is due to the rich who have worked diligently and honestly to attain their status and who are generous to share their wealth in order to alleviate the plight of the poor and needy. But beyond these positive instances, might corruption be the reason behind the ever-increasing gap between the rich and poor in the world?

I would contend that it is.

First, we can learn from an organization like Transparency International about the degree of corruption in various countries around the world. Transparency International is a global advocacy network that fights corruption through local chapters in more than ninety countries by seeking the cooperation of concerned people in government, society, business, and media. In 2010, Transparency International released a survey that ranked one hundred seventy-eight countries in order from the least corrupt to the most corrupt using their Corruption Perception Indicator (CPI).[2]

When we review this survey alongside the World Fact Book maintained by the CIA on the purchasing power per capita of more than two hundred countries in the world,[3] we discover that the countries ranked as the most corrupt, according to the CPI, are also the most poor, according to the World Fact Book. Even the ranking order of the countries perceived to be the most corrupt closely matches the ranking order of those with the highest poverty levels.

These two publications, when considered side by side, show that the degree of poverty in a country is directly proportional to its level of corruption. The more rampant corruption is in a country, the more poverty its people suffer, and vice versa.

Various organizations, institutions, and even governments have risen to the call to address the evils of this social disease. Some of these organizations, institutions, and anti-corruption groups are referenced in chapter twelve of this book. These groups have conducted observations of the occurrences of corruption and have recommended anti-corruption measures to prevent or at least minimize the occurrences of corruption in order to curtail its growth in most countries having these problems.

These are good steps taken in the fight against corruption because any step taken to address the evils of corruption is progress toward minimizing its negative impact on government and the governed. However, in spite of the sincere efforts and active campaigns and involvement of these organizations in this issue, it seems the fight for corruption has a long, long way to go.

Discoveries of the corruption often come late, just like a diagnosis of cancer often comes in the advanced stage of the malady. Corruption is discovered only after it has impacted people's lives, the government, other countries, and the world.

Corruption is a continuing phenomenon. It has been in existence since the fall of Adam, and it is powered by covetousness and greed. As we shall see, corruption starts to grow and spawn in the hearts of men.

The Octopus

A study of the nature, characteristics, and behavioral habits of an octopus will give you a better understanding of corruption and the Corruptor.

The octopus is a creature that lives in the depths of the sea. It is a predator and a nomadic creature. One species of octopus is very small, but another species of octopus grows big, is fast, and increases in weight as it feeds on its victims.

The octopus moves gracefully. Its tentacles are lithe but powerful, and it can fight even sharks with its tentacles. The octopus has various ways to catch its unsuspecting prey with its long, lithe tentacles. Its supple body can squeeze itself into tight spaces to catch food. It can make itself appear as part of its surroundings by changing its skin color. It can distort its tentacles in a manner similar to a human arm. It can even change itself to look like other sea creatures by matching their colors, shapes, and forms.

The octopus can obscure itself to trick its would-be victim. It can copy the look and form of other sea creatures to deceive its predator or prey. It can even make itself look like a harmless coral or rock laying on the seabed—and it can do all these amazing things in a split second.[4]

In addition, the octopus has a secret weapon: ink. It can shoot ink out of its funnel to hide itself in a back cloud of water. What's more, the ink contains chemical properties that attack the sense of smell and taste to confuse its enemy or victim.[5]

The octopus is a very intelligent creature with a highly organized brain. It possesses an intricate nervous system that is very responsive to its environment. It uses human-like eyes to locate its prey. Recent findings suggest that the tentacles of the octopus may have its own intellectual ability and nervous system. Its tentacles can, by their own will, work by themselves after receiving a command from the "main brain" of the octopus.[6]

Just like the octopus, Satan is a deceiver and a predator. He is an intelligent being, and he is a beautiful but fallen angel. He can present himself in many ways and in many forms to his intended victims. He can even show them he is like them—harmless and trustworthy. He can change himself to appear as an angel of light (2 Cor. 11:14). He manages a host of demons to deceive, tempt, and enslave men into corruption. He is very subtle and a great pretender so that he can entrap you in his evil schemes.

He has secret weapons, too. He can create confusion in the mind of a victim through lies and deception so they will not be able to think clearly and will easily succumb to temptation. He also moves from place to place, hunting good ground for his operation in order to establish corruption in the hearts of men.

UNDERSTANDING CORRUPTION'S ORIGIN

In order to defeat corruption, we have to thoroughly understand its origin, nature, and ways. How did it begin? Does it really have a beginning? Who originated it? Who is the power behind it?

To answer these questions, let's go back and look at a point in time in eternity. God is "the Alpha and the Omega, the Beginning and the End…who is and who was and who is to come, the Almighty" (Rev. 1:8). God is a holy God who inhabits eternity (Isa. 57:15). He created angels who serve Him for His purposes (Ps. 103:20).

Among those angels was an angel named Lucifer, who was "the seal of perfection, full of wisdom and perfect in beauty" (Ezek. 28:12). But because of Lucifer's beauty, the heart of this angel was lifted up. He *corrupted* his wisdom for the sake of his beauty (v. 17).

The book of Isaiah describes how Lucifer fell:

> "How you are fallen from heaven, O Lucifer,
> son of the morning! How you are cut down
> to the ground, you who weakened the nations!
> For you have said in your heart: '*I will* ascend
> into heaven, *I will* exalt my throne above the
> stars of God; *I will* also sit on the mount of
> the congregation on the farthest sides of the
> north; *I will* ascend above the heights of the
> clouds, *I will* be like the Most High.'"
>
> —ISAIAH 14:12–14, EMPHASIS ADDED

The footnote of this passage in the *New Scofield Study Bible* says Lucifer "evidently refers to Satan—the prince of this world system. His sin pointed to the beginning of sin in the universe; when Satan said, 'will' sin begun."[7] Satan decided in his heart to sin, as he asserted "I will" five times in his rebellion against the God who created him and for whom he was created.

So corruption actually began at a point in time in eternity. It began at the point when Satan rebelled against the Most High God.

Satan corrupted himself by coveting God's exalted position, power, reign, and authority over the universe. He wanted to usurp all that God is and was and forever will be. He wanted to exalt himself above the God he was created to serve. He corrupted himself by the sins of covetousness, pride, and rebellion, and he was able to win a host of angels to join him in his rebellion. These angels have been reserved by God in everlasting chains under darkness for the judgment of the great day (Jude 1:6).

God is a holy God (Lev. 19:2). His throne is in heaven, where He rules over all the heavens and the earth (Isa. 66:1). Heaven, too, is a holy place (Ps. 48:1), and sin cannot be where God is. Therefore, because of his sin, Satan was cast out of heaven. The other angels who took sides with him in his rebellion against God were also cast out of heaven and down to earth.

But Satan and his demons did not give up without a fight:

> And war broke out in heaven: Michael [a chief angel of God] and his angels, fought with the dragon [Satan]; and the dragon and his angels fought, but they did not prevail, nor was a place found for them in heaven any longer. So the great dragon was cast out, that serpent of old, called the Devil and Satan, who deceives the whole world; he was cast to the earth, and his angels were cast out with him.
>
> —REVELATION 12:7–9

Satan rules in this world as the prince of the power of the air (Eph. 2:2). Together with his demons, Satan works in the hearts of men with corrupt minds who are "lovers of themselves, lovers of money, boasters, proud, blasphemers, disobedient to parents, unthankful, unholy, unloving, unforgiving, slanderers, without self-control, brutal, despisers of good, traitors, headstrong, haughty, lovers of pleasure rather than lovers of God, having a form of godliness but denying its power" (2 Tim. 3:2–5). These men are easy prey for Satan. He can catch them easily to give in to temptation and desire to obey his corruptive ways, and therefore to be enslaved by corruption.

Satan is truly the first Corruptor and the author of all corruption.

Adam and Eve

God created Adam in His own image—in the likeness of the Father, the Son, and the Holy Spirit. He also created a suitable helper for Adam in his wife, Eve. Then God gave Adam dominion over the fish of the sea, the birds of the air, and the cattle. He gave him dominion over all the earth and over every creeping thing that creeps on the earth (Gen. 1:26–27).

God purposed Adam to have the authority over all the earth and everything in it. He gave Adam everything he needed to live a carefree life. He made Adam the CEO of everything He had created on the earth. He wanted Adam to enjoy his life in the garden, which was like paradise on earth.

It may be safe to visualize that all the creatures God created were in meek submission to Adam and Eve. Adam and Eve lived with all these creatures in a peaceful and mutual coexistence. They were familiar with each other. Adam gave names to all the cattle, the birds of the air, and every beast of the field. Whatever Adam called each living creature, that was its name (Gen. 2:19–20).

But soon Adam's perfect existence in Eden was interrupted by Satan, who hid himself in the body of the graceful serpent. Satan confused Eve with his words, saying, "Has God indeed said, 'You shall not eat of every tree of the garden'?" (Gen. 3:1). Satan, speaking through the serpent, twisted the word of God.

He succeeded in creating confusion in Eve's mind, and therefore Eve answered him: "We may eat the fruit of the trees of the garden; but of the fruit of the tree which is in the midst of the garden, God has said, 'You shall not eat it, *nor shall you touch it,* lest you die'" (vv. 2–3, emphasis added). Eve modified God's command by adding words of her own—"nor shall you touch it"—showing that she was really confused. Thus, the serpent succeeded in sowing doubt in Eve's mind about God's command, and he eventually deceived her with his lies.

Next, the serpent worked on Eve's senses of sight and taste and activated pride within her, which caused her to desire to eat the fruit of the tree of the knowledge of good and evil. She believed what Satan told her, that if she ate the forbidden fruit she would not die but instead know how to differentiate between evil and good like God. The fruit looked so good to eat (vv. 4–6), and maybe Eve thought, "Why not? Anyway, God said all the fruit in the garden is our food to eat."

As Eve pondered this, she saw that the appearance of the fruit belied what God had said to Adam: "But of the tree of the knowledge of good and evil you shall not eat, for in the day that you eat of it you shall surely die" (Gen. 2:17). Maybe she thought God had commanded only Adam not to eat of that fruit. Maybe she forgot she was of one body with Adam, for God made her out of a rib taken from Adam while he slept (vv. 21–22).

Eve was tempted to be wise like God to know the difference between good and evil. The appearance of the fruit appealed to her sense of sight, and she craved the taste of it because it looked so good to eat. She entertained her desire to be wise like God, and Eve's desire gave birth to sin when she picked the fruit from the tree and ate it. She also gave the fruit to Adam, who forgot God's command not to eat the fruit and its consequence of death. Eve was deceived, and Adam disobeyed God's command.

By willfully eating the forbidden fruit, Adam committed his first sin against God. Consequently, Adam and Eve were banished from Eden (Gen. 3:22–24). Adam lost his authority of dominion over all the earth, and Satan usurped and gained control over the authority God had given to Adam for the management of the earth and everything in it.

When Adam sinned, his nature, which had been created in the image of the Triune God, was tweaked by the corrupted nature of Satan. Adam absorbed for himself and his descendants Satan's corrupted nature—and all of us inherited this sinful nature from Adam:

> Therefore, just as through one man [Adam] sin entered the world, and death through sin, and thus death spread to all men, because all sinned.
>
> —ROMANS 5:12

It's been said that corruption has been around the world for about six thousand years.[8] But in the days of Noah, the ninth generation after Adam, the Bible says, "The earth also was corrupt before God, and the earth was filled with violence. So God looked upon the earth, and indeed it was corrupt; for *all flesh* had corrupted their way on the earth" (Gen. 6:11–12, emphasis added). Cain, Adam's first-born son, committed the first murder on earth by killing his younger brother Abel (Gen. 4:8) "because his works were evil and his brother's righteous" (1 John 3:12).

Ever since the first sin on the earth, Adam's sinful nature has been carried down the bloodline of Adam's descendants, the entire human race. As we are all descended from Adam, you have his sinful nature, and so do I. We are carriers of Adam's DNA, and that makes us prone to temptation and sin, for "all have sinned and fall short of the glory of God" (Rom. 3:23).

Satan failed to usurp God's authority, power, and majesty when rebelling against Him in heaven. When he was cast out of heaven, Satan succeeded by deceiving and lying to Eve and usurping Adam's God-given authority to rule with dominion over all the earth.

However, Satan's usurpation of Adam's dominion on earth is only until a time determined by God. The apostle John describes how Satan will be dealt with at that time:

> Then I saw an angel coming down from heaven, having the key to the bottomless pit and a great chain in his hand. He laid hold of the dragon, that serpent of old, who is the Devil and Satan, and bound him for a thousand years; and he cast him into the bottomless pit, and shut him up, and set a seal on him, so that he should deceive the nations no more till the thousand years were finished. But after these things he must be released for a little while.
>
> —REVELATION 20:1–3

Here on the earth, Satan continues to fight against the Almighty God by trying to establish full control over mankind and the earth. He tries to do this by working in the hearts of men—in our sinful nature that we received from Adam's tweaked DNA. But we have also a godly nature, as we were created in the image of the Triune God. However, because Adam's tweaked DNA is in us, we are also capable of doing good or evil as we choose to do.

Satan is the ruler of the world system we live in. Therefore, he will try to do all he can to tempt, harm, destroy, and separate you from God and prevent God's good plan for your future with Him in heaven. Satan is against God and everything good God is doing and has purposed to do for you. Like a thief, Satan does not come except "to steal, and to kill, and to destroy," but Jesus "[has] come that [you] may have life, and that [you] may have it more abundantly" (John 10:10).

As Satan coveted the glory, power, and authority of God, he also would like to receive glory from your corrupted ways instead of allowing you to give the glory to God by your righteous living. Satan will do everything he can to ensnare you in his evil trap. He wants you to be his prisoner to obey his commands to do evil and everything wrong. He wants to turn you into his robot to obey him by downloading all things evil into your mind until you put those evil thoughts into action. He will deceive you into thinking you are doing the right thing.

Satan wants you to worship and obey him instead of God. He wants to steal you away from God and His glorious plans and blessings for you. He wants to establish himself as your god and receive your worship through the evil works he makes you do for him. He is bent on doing this because he is the god of this present world and because he wants to establish corruption in your life and in the world.

Here is how it works with Satan, the great and corrupt octopus. He will tempt you with things of the world that arouse "the lust of the flesh, the lust of the eyes, and the pride of life" (1 John 2:16)—things that boost your pride and lift your self-esteem and are of this world. Money, the luxuries money can buy, power, illegal things, material things, things of pleasure, vanity, and things that boost your pride. The Corruptor will use as bait those things that appeal to your senses of touch, sight, hearing, smell, taste, and pride to ensnare you in sin and corruption.

Corruption usually lurks in places where there is a need for supply and demand—in our daily living. But mostly it lurks where authority and money are used to transact business, in an exchange of need and supply or provision. It visits governments and private places where big transactions occur, and it visits homes and the marketplace. It visits institutions too.

It can strike anywhere, anytime. It can establish itself so easily, as long as there are people who can be deceived—notably, those who lack knowledge or discernment and succumb to the temptations presented, and those who are potential deceivers and corrupters themselves. Most people are usually destroyed for lack of knowledge (Hos. 4:6).

Once established, corruption grows so fast, as it fills the corrupted of its wages. Corruption devours. It is never satisfied. It is addictive. It is also like cancer, growing beyond control. It affects everything good, turning it bad. It is decadent.

Eventually, it seeps like water through a small opening in a dike, seeking its way forward until it succeeds in breaking families, societies, and authorities from the norms of conduct and away from respect for people's God-given rights. Corruption becomes a way of life for everyone and eventually a norm in the culture.

The seed of corruption is easily planted and grows in the hearts of men because it thrives in our sinful nature. Mankind is not easily content but seeks more and more of the wealth, material goods, and prestige of this world. When we concern ourselves with gaining something beyond our need in order to feed our lust and pride, we are an easy target for the work of corruption. But can you overcome it? That's what we'll discover next.

Chapter 4

CAN YOU OVERCOME
CORRUPTION?

Although God created man in His image, man is weak because he is of the earth, formed from the dust of the ground. As a lump of earth easily crumbles to the touch, so do we easily succumb to the temptations of sin and corruption. We are the perfect prey for Satan's evil plan of corruption. Our physical nature and our sinful nature have made us highly susceptible to the temptations of the Corruptor.

This means you are easily tempted by the bait the Corruptor uses to corrupt you. He knows the condition of your heart because Adam's weakness is now your weakness. Just as in your physical makeup you are prone to contracting the same diseases your ancestors had, so are you also prone to temptation and sin like Adam, your spiritual ancestor, was:

> For the flesh lusts against the Spirit, and the Spirit against the flesh; and these are contrary to one another, so that you do not do the things that you wish.
>
> —GALATIANS 5:17

Also, the apostle Paul wrote:

> But sin, taking opportunity…produced in me all manner of evil desire…. For what I am doing, I do not understand. For what I will to do, that I do not practice; but what I hate, that I do.
>
> —ROMANS 7:8, 15

But you are not totally hopeless. Whatever damage the evil one did to give you Adam's sinful nature, it was not enough to erase the stamp of God's image in you. As God the Father, He is the provider of all your needs and your protector (Matt. 6:11, 13). Being created from the dust of the ground, your framework is always in a state of weakness. The flesh is weak (Matt. 26:41), which makes it difficult for you to live a life of obedience and righteousness in God.

Therefore God made sure One who is greater and stronger than you but who could identify with you and feel what you are going through—God the Son, the second person of the Godhead—was with Him when Adam was created. God the Son was present and worked as One with the Triune God in creating man in God's likeness. He also came in the flesh to live on the earth as the Son of Man in the person of Jesus. He was perfect God and perfect Man and lived on the earth a perfectly sinless life.

Jesus is a High Priest who can sympathize with your weaknesses because He was in all points tempted as you are, yet was without sin (Heb. 4:15). The Lord is very compassionate and merciful (James 5:11), and He is "able to save to the uttermost those who come to God through Him, since He always lives to make intercession for them" (Heb. 7:25).

Knowing how weak man is, the Spirit of the living God—who also was present with the Triune God when God created man in His image—is here to help, to guide, to strengthen, and to minister to you, *but only if you will allow Him to do so*:

> Likewise the Spirit also helps in [your] weaknesses. For [you] do not know what [you] should pray for as [you] ought, but the Spirit Himself makes intercession for [you] with groanings which cannot be uttered. Now He who searches the hearts knows what the mind of the Spirit is, because He makes intercession for [those made righteous] according to the will of God.
>
> —Romans 8:26–27

Despite the curse of corruption and death that Adam's sin brought upon man, whatever God had purposed for man stands because His faithfulness endures to all generations (Ps. 119:90). God purposed to create man in His image, and He did (Gen. 1:26–27). God desires you to come to Him (Matt. 11:28), to restore you to Himself, and to lead you in the paths of righteousness (Ps. 23:3) so you can live the life He has purposed for you (John 10:10).

Although Satan succeeded in corrupting Adam's godly image, God's purpose for man cannot be undone. Because of the Father's great love for us, He provided a way to undo Satan's influence by sending His Son as a perfect sacrifice for you and for all. Jesus was led to the cross "as a lamb to the slaughter, and as a sheep before its shearers is silent, so He opened not His mouth" (Isa. 53:7) to die for you, as a propitiation for your corruption, my corruption, and the corruption of the whole world (1 John 2:2).

Because God does not change, you are not consumed (Mal. 3:6). God is a loving God, and He showed His love for you in that while you were still a sinner, Jesus Christ died for you (Rom. 5:8). Jesus offered his perfect, sinless body to take the brunt, the punishment, the scourges, and the pain that you deserved for your corrupted and sinful life. He Himself bore on His sinless body your infirmities and iniquities. And He can empower you to overcome corruption because of His finished, atoning sacrifice for you on the cross—*if* you submit your life to Him.

Jesus nailed all your sins with Him on the cross—your corrupted works are on His hands and your corrupted ways are on His feet. The crown of thorns pricked His head. He took on the arrows of the wicked one that were aimed at your mind, and He prevailed.

And yet to further reinforce His work of salvation, Jesus shed His blood, His very life, to flow from His side for your redemption (John 19:34). His blood redeemed you from the hand of the enemy. Only the power of His atoning blood can wash your sins away, "not by works of righteousness which [you] have done" (Tit. 3:5). Jesus paid it once for you and all men.

God is able to bring back and re-create again your godly nature, which was tweaked by Adam's sin, into His image, the image of His Son, Jesus. Only believe in the Lord Jesus Christ and what He has done on the cross for you, and you will be saved from corruption: "But as many as received Him, to them He gave the right to become children of God, to those who believe in His name" (John 1:12; see also Acts 16:31).

What a wonderful Father you have to secure for you all these things that He has done by the offering of the body and life-blood of Jesus, His Son! What Jesus has done is perfectly sealed by the presence of the Holy Spirit, the third Person of the Godhead, whom the Father had sent (2 Cor. 1:22). The sacrifice of Jesus at the cross of Calvary is finished, complete, and perfect. It is only through your faith in Jesus and His finished atoning sacrifice at the cross that you can overcome the evils of corruption in the world (1 John 5:4).

If you are in Jesus and have surrendered your life to Him, then He has become for you "wisdom from God—and righteousness and sanctification and redemption" (1 Cor. 1:30) from the corruption of sin that leads to death into a life of victory.

How can you gain this life? Listen! "The spirit of a man is the lamp of the Lord, searching all the inner depths of his heart" (Prov. 20:27). The Lord forms the spirit within you (Zech. 12:1). This means the spirit of man can receive revelations from the Spirit of the living God, whether that man is submitted to God and living his life in God's will or not. Even if you are in rebellion against God, He will speak words of life, of love, and of comfort to you: "He will guide you into all truth... and He will tell you things to come" (John 16:13).

God may speak in one way or another to you, yet you may not understand it. He may speak to you in a dream or a vision in the night while you sleep. He will open your ears to instruct you or to warn you to turn away from the ways of corruption. He will keep you safe from the pit and turn you back to Him.

God sometimes speaks when you are in great pain—even when your life seems like it is being drawn to death—for in pain, a promise of hope is a welcome relief.

Sometimes God sends a messenger with a word from Him. God speaks clearly and confirms what He is saying to you by His Word. If you will listen to Him, He will deliver your life from the destruction of corruption. (See Job 33:14–24.)

We are sinners, you and I, and we are destined to die physically and spiritually because of the sin we inherited from Adam and which is made even more complicated by our own unrighteousness. Yet God "is longsuffering toward [you], not willing that [you] should perish [be corrupted] but that [you] should come to repentance" (2 Pet. 3:9).

God's desire is to establish His kingdom in your heart and in your life. He wants to bless you and prosper you and give you a life that is free from covetousness and that "does not consist in the abundance of the things [you] possess" (Luke 12:15). Jesus came "that [you] may have life, and that [you] may have it more abundantly" (John 10:10).

The things of the world are used as bait by the devil to corrupt you. His purpose is to catch you and make you fall captive to his corruptive influence. Satan and his demon spirits are always on the lookout for victims. They observe everything that is happening in the world and in people's lives. They listen to the words of your mouth, as every word you speak reveals the condition of your heart and helps them determine if you will make a possible candidate to work with him as a slave of his corruptive schemes. Your words reveal who you are, for the words which proceed out of your mouth come from your heart, and they defile you (Prov. 27:19; Matt. 15:18). You should be careful of the words you speak, for they carry the power of a blessing or a curse, which the evil spirits are waiting to hear you speak.

Could you overcome the evils of corruption? The answer is yes—you can, if you have faith in Jesus' sacrifice on the cross and the power of His blood shed for your redemption:

> For God so loved the world that He gave His only begotten Son, that if you believe in Him, you shall not perish but have everlasting life. God did not send His Son into the world to condemn the world, but that the world through Him might be saved from corruption and death.
> —JOHN 3:16–17, AUTHOR'S PARAPHRASE

Also, the apostle Peter wrote:

> Grace and peace be multiplied to you in the knowledge of God and of Jesus our Lord, as His divine power has given us all things that pertain to life and godliness, through the knowledge of Him who called us by glory and virtue, by which have been given to us exceedingly great and precious promises, that through these you may be partakers of the

divine nature, having escaped the *corruption* that is in the world through lust.

—2 PETER 1:2–4, EMPHASIS ADDED

Remember, in the world, you will always have tribulation, but if you have entrusted your life to Jesus, you will have victory over the corruption that is the work of Satan. Jesus said, "'These things I have spoken to you, that in Me you may have peace. In the world you will have tribulation; but be of good cheer, I have overcome the world'" (John 16:33).

Chapter 5

WAYS
CORRUPTION WORKS

CORRUPTION, AS A state of rottenness, operates in many ways. Its ways are as varied as there are ways to adapt to situations in people's lives and circumstances. Below are some of the ways corruption establishes its control in the places and people or groups of people it intends to victimize to obey its schemes.

BRIBERY

Bribery happens when someone who, for his own selfish advantage, offers a lure to another person in order to persuade that person to do illegal things or to participate in something wrong. Instead of submitting to a legal process or morally established procedures, the person makes a tempting offer to another person who has the capacity to make their desire come to pass. When that person accepts the offer of a bribe or even just consents to agree to the condition of the bribe, there's an implied agreement that he will do the will of the one bribing him. This "man accepts the bribe behind the back to pervert the ways of justice" (Prov. 17:23).

The corruptor and the corrupted in this scenario are both motivated by selfish gain without respect or concern for established principles or the well-being and rights of others. Both parties agree on an unwritten condition of the bribery scheme. The illegal or immoral activity is supposed to be hidden and untraceable. The parties barter one's selfish interest against the other's selfish gain without regard to the rules of law, procedures, moral principles, and the rights and well-being of others.

Wikipedia defines bribery as "a form of corruption, is an act implying money or gift given that alters the behavior of the recipient. Bribery constitutes a crime and is defined by *Black's Law Dictionary* as the offering, giving, receiving, or soliciting of any item of value to influence the actions of an official or other persons in charge of a public or legal duty."[1]

Merriam-Webster's Dictionary defines bribery as "the act or practice of giving or taking a bribe"[2] and defines bribe as "money or favor given or promised in order to influence the judgment or conduct of a person in a position of trust; something that serves to induce or influence."[3]

There are two forms of bribery—active and passive—especially noted in the political arena:

"Active bribery...[is] the promising, offering or giving by any person, directly or indirectly, of any undue advantage [to any public official], for himself or herself or for anyone else, for him or her to act or refrain from acting in the exercise of his or her functions.... Passive bribery can be defined as the request or receipt [by any public official], directly or indirectly, of any undue advantage, for himself or herself or for anyone else, or the acceptance of an offer or a promise of such an advantage, to act or refrain from acting in the exercise of his or her functions."[4]

A bribe has the power to pervert justice. It can make one show partiality, blind the eyes of the discerning, and pervert the words of the righteous. A bribe corrupts the heart (Deut. 16:19).

A bribe can come in many forms. It can be a desired action, special treatment, or thing of value that influences the action, decision, or conduct of a person in a position of trust or in a position of power or responsibility to do or to give:

The bribe is the gift bestowed to influence the recipient's conduct. It may be any money, good, right in action, property, preferment, privilege, emolument, object of value, advantage, or merely a promise or undertaking to induce or influence the action, vote, or influence of a person in an official or public capacity.[5]

Three Examples of Bribery in the Bible

Before the start of His ministry as the Son of Man, Jesus fasted in the wilderness for forty days. During that time, Satan tried to offer Him a bribe of all the kingdoms of the world and their glory in exchange for being worshipped. But Jesus, who is God, cannot be tempted with evil (James 1:13). And Jesus used the Word of God to rebuke the devil, saying, "Away with you, Satan! For it is written, 'You shall worship the Lord your God, and Him only you shall serve.' Then the devil left Him, and behold, angels came and ministered to Him" (Matt. 4:10–11).

Another incidence of bribery occurred near the end of Jesus' three-year ministry on the earth. Judas, one of the twelve disciples of the Lord, was corrupted and went to the chief priests to ask them how much they would be willing to give him if he delivered Jesus to them. The priests counted thirty pieces of silver to Judas. And from that time on, Satan, the Corruptor, lorded it over Judas as "he sought opportunity to betray Him" (Matt. 26:16).

It's hard for us to grasp how Judas, who had been a disciple of the Lord for almost three years, had heard His teachings about God and the kingdom of God with his own ears, and who saw the many miracles Jesus did with his own eyes, could be corrupted by a bribe of thirty pieces of silver. Could Judas have forgotten having seen the Lord bless five loaves of bread and two fish to miraculously feed five thousand hungry men? Could he have forgotten that twelve baskets of fragments remained? If Judas had a need, surely the Lord Jesus could provide it. He had seen miracles happen before his eyes. The blind could see and the lame could walk; lepers were cleansed and the deaf could hear; the dead were raised and the poor were given the gospel.

Judas' love of money led him to betray the Lord. He was the treasurer of Jesus' ministry group. He kept the money box and often took what was put into it (John 12:6). He was like one whose "desire to be rich" led him to "fall into temptation and a snare" to ask for the bribe (1 Tim. 6:9). His "love of money" planted the "root of all kinds of evil," such as greediness in his heart to stray from the Lord Jesus and betray him (v. 10).

If Judas, a disciple of Jesus, could be corrupted, there is a strong possibility you could also be corrupted. Therefore, it is good to take heed, if you think you stand strong against temptation, lest you fall (1 Cor. 10:12).

Lastly, after His death on the cross, Jesus was buried in a tomb hewn out of rock, which was sealed with a stone. Soldiers were assigned to guard the tomb to prevent His disciples from stealing His body. After three days, Jesus rose from the dead. When the guards saw the empty tomb, they reported it to the chief priests, and the priests gave the soldiers a large amount of money to lie and say, "His disciples took Him away while they slept." (See Matthew 28:11–15.)

A bribe can be anything that arouses an instinct in man to covet. It can be something pleasing to your eyes, something that indulges or fulfills the cravings of your flesh, or something that boosts your self-esteem and exalts you in the eyes of others—all these are known as "the lust of the flesh, the lust of the eyes, and the pride of life" (1 John 2:16).

Bribery also gives the corruptor illegal gain or advantage over the legal interest or well-being of others and compels the corrupted to distort the normal, legal, and moral way of doing things in order to illegally gain something for himself. The corrupted does this without due regard to what is right or the interest of those living righteously and obeying the rules.

It isn't unusual to read and hear stories about people caught in the mess of corruption, and they have often been corrupted with bribes involving money, pleasure, riches, and the big things money can buy. In chapter ten, I will tell the story of my friend who overcame the attempts to bribe and corrupt her in the course of her work, which involved the preparation of estimates, prequalifying contractors, evaluating bid proposals, and writing recommendations for the award of contracts. Workers of corruption tried to tempt her with a bribe of a big amount of money.

The wrong offer came at the perfect time for tempting her, for she needed tuition money badly for her children. Her savings was gone and she was not earning enough for their needs. She was in a vulnerable situation at a vulnerable time. It is only by the grace of God that she was able to overcome the temptation of the corruptor. Her fear of the Lord helped deliver her out of the evil of corruption (Prov. 16:6).

"GREASE MONEY" OR "GREASING"

The practice of greasing usually happens to facilitate transactions, such as applications for licenses or permits, in order to keep an application moving fast and avoiding bureaucratic red tape.[6] This practice feeds on greed or the love of money on the part of the person receiving the "grease," and the "greaser" who offers money or something of value gains undue advantage over other applicants who are waiting in line for their turn. This corruptive practice often happens where there is a bureaucracy at work in an organization—where there is "an unwieldy administrative system burdened with excessive complexity and lack of flexibility."[7]

"PAYOLA"

The word *payola* was introduced into the English language through the music industry. It refers to "the paying of cash or gifts in exchange for airplay" and is "a contraction of the words 'pay' and 'Victrola' (LP record player)."[8] On May 9, 1960, a disc jocky named Alan Freed was indicted for accepting $2,500 for playing certain records on air. After his trial, "the anti-payola statute was passed under which payola became a misdemeanor, penalty by up to $10,000 in fines and one year in prison."[9]

COLLUSION

Merriam-Webster's Dictionary defines collusion as a "secret agreement or cooperation especially for an illegal or deceitful purpose." It may happen in any organization—government, public, or private—and, just like other forms of corruption, remains unwritten to hide the trail of the illegal transaction.

Collusion may occur in connection with the procurement activities of an organization. A bidder may solicit the connivance of other bidders to submit bids that make it appear the ambitious bidder had submitted the lowest bid among all the bidders. This is done so that the lowest bidder will be awarded a contract.

The bidders involved in the collusion process effectively circumvent the tendering process, making it appear legal and in order. All of these bidders are guilty of committing fraud. The organization that receives a rigged bid ends up paying more than the fair cost of material or services because the lowest bid was padded to pay everyone who participated in the bid process.

This may not seem like a way of corruption, but the bidders corrupt the procurement process by committing fraud against the organization calling for bids. This is collusion, and the motivation is greed. The deception suits the purposes of all the colluding bidders: "They devise iniquities: 'We have perfected a shrewd scheme.' Both the inward thought and the heart of man is deep" (Ps. 64:6). These are like the men the apostle Paul wrote about the last days, saying, "Evil men and impostors will grow worse and worse, deceiving and being deceived" (2 Tim. 3:13).

EXTORTION OR COERCION

Wikipedia describes extortion as "a criminal offense when a person unlawfully obtains either money, property or services from a person(s), entity, or institution, through coercion"[10] and describes coercion as "the practice of compelling a person or manipulating them to behave in an involuntary way (whether through action or inaction) by use of threats, intimidation, trickery, or some other form of pressure or force. These are used as leverage, to force the victims to act in the desired way."[11]

Extortion in this sense not only encourages corruption but also nourishes and fuels its growth. As people, because of fear, give in to the demands of the extortionist, it makes the extortionist more arrogant, fierce, forceful, and dangerous. People who observe such things often close their eyes and shut their mouths for fear of retaliation from the extortionist. Victims and witnesses passively accept extortion or coercion in order to preserve their lives and businesses. They accept extortion as a contingency cost of their lives and as a necessary evil in society.

Businesses, merchants, or suppliers of goods and services give in to extortion practices in the processes related to their businesses, such as testing, certification, approval, shipping, and delivery to consumers. We often hear of news about the rigging of tenders, vote-buying during elections, or simply intimidation of any sort related to the manufacturing and delivery of goods, products, and services.

The costs incurred because of extortion are added to the cost of products or services delivered to consumers or clients. The consumers then bear this added cost. Therefore, the people actually subsidize the cost of extortion by paying its value-added cost for the products and services they need.

Extortion not only causes an increase in the cost of products and services. It also impacts the quality, extent, value, and measure of commodities and services provided. We actually pay more to receive less or substandard goods, commodities, and services. In view of this, the people suffer even more.

The cycle of corruption through extortion, which keeps repeating itself, is an unbreakable cycle. It perhaps contributes to the increased cost of living and the plunging level of poverty in the world. The unscrupulous become rich while the poor become more poor. But the Lord sees the way of those who increase this burden on people's lives: "'You take usury and increase; you have made profit from your neighbors by extortion, and have forgotten Me'" (Ezek. 22:12).

Manipulation

The objective in manipulation is to gain immoral or undue personal benefit or advantage for one's self or on behalf of others. This usually happens within an organization among those having direct involvement in the conduct of a business process. It may happen without anyone else knowing. A person in authority can impose his power on the exercise of the business contrary to regulations or laws that govern its function and operation. Or, as in the case of private businesses, an officer may exercise his prerogative in accordance with the charter of the corporation and with the passive agreement of other officials privy to the gain. Or in the case of an individual in an organization, he can do it by himself, acting alone or with the agreement or knowledge of others. He only needs to have responsibility for, access to, or authority over the matter being manipulated.

In the first instance, a person who holds higher authority may pressure a subordinate to make decisions contrary to established laws, regulations, or procedures governing that organization in the matter of contracts or in the processing of any transaction within the jurisdiction of that organization. This person's actions are meant to suit his own purposes, and he will attain it by exercising undue pressure, even to the extent of messing up or corrupting the right thing needing to be done. This person may be doing it for his own benefit or to the advantage or favor of someone else. It can sometimes be done to return a past favor.

In the private sector, however, the authorized official does not need to use pressure or manipulation to obtain his desire. Within the confines of his work structure, an officer needs only to persuade his peers to agree to his plan, which is provided in the bylaws of the organization, so he can easily manipulate the situation to favor his objective. He and his peers who are also benefitting are acting in accordance with the rules of the organization. It is only when the use of this power grows out of bounds because of greed that corruption begins.

Data and reports concerning a business operation can

also be manipulated by those who have the access to it in order to hide losses and reflect good performance. This can be done to deceive investors or persons who have an interest in the organization. It can also be done by higher officials in order to save their skins.

Example of Manipulation in the Bible

The Bible tells the story of how Jacob, Isaac's son and Abraham's grandson, stole the birthright blessing from Esau, his older brother, who was the firstborn son. (See Genesis 25 and 27.)

Jacob and Esau were twins born to Isaac and Rebekah. As the twins grew, Esau became a skillful hunter and man of the field, but Jacob was gentle and dwelled in tents. Isaac loved Esau because he ate of his game, but Rebekah loved Jacob (Gen. 25:27–28).

During that time, Isaac was already old and his eyes were dim so that he could not see. One day, Isaac had a longing for Esau's stew, so he called him and told him to hunt and cook a stew from his game so he could eat and bless Esau before he dies. Rebekah was listening to their conversation and hatched a plan to manipulate Isaac's plan so that Jacob, her favorite son, would inherit the blessing of her husband. (A father's blessing was so important to Isaac's people, especially during those days.)

So Rebekah instructed Jacob to bring her two choice

kids of the goats. She then prepared and cooked Isaac's favorite dish for Jacob to bring to his father. Rebekah then tooked Esau's favorite clothes and let Jacob wear them. She put the skins of the kids of the goats on Jacobs's hands and on the smooth part of his neck, and then she sent Jacob to bring the savory food and the bread which she had prepared to his father. So Jacob brought the food to Isaac.

Isaac wondered how Esau found the game so quickly, and he asked Jacob who he was. Jacob lied to his father and said he was Esau. Isaac asked Jacob to come closer to him in order to confirm if he really was Esau. Isaac felt the hairy skin of Jacob's arms from the goat's skin, and although Isaac heard the voice of Jacob but felt Esau in Jacob's hairy hands, he was satisfied Jacob was "Esau" indeed.

Isaac ate the food brought to him by Jacob and drank the wine he gave him. After eating, Isaac asked Jacob to come near him to kiss his father. Isaac smelled the smell of Esau's clothing that Jacob was wearing and blessed Jacob.

Just after Isaac had finished blessing Jacob, Esau came with the savory food that he had cooked from his hunting and brought it to his father, Isaac. In that moment, Isaac knew he had blessed his younger son, who had deceived him because of Rebekah's manipulation and succeeded in stealing the blessing from Esau.

Therefore, "Esau hated Jacob because of the [stolen]

blessing with which his father blessed him, and Esau said in his heart, 'The days of mourning for my father are at hand; then I will kill my brother Jacob'" (Gen. 27:41).

The Bible says that when Rebekah was pregnant in her womb with the twins, the two struggled together inside her womb. When she inquired of the Lord, He said to her, "Two nations are in your womb, two peoples shall be separated from your body; one people shall be stronger than the other, and the older shall serve the younger" (Gen. 25:23).

Also, before the case of the stolen blessing, Esau had already sold his birthright to Jacob to ease his weariness and hunger with a bowl of stew he requested from Jacob when he came home from hunting. Esau agreed to give his birthright to Jacob in exchange for this bowl of fleshly gratification. He despised his own birthright. (See Genesis 25:29–33.)

TAMPERING, DISTORTION, AND FALSIFICATION

For anyone who has access to records in a place of work, there is a strong temptation to take advantage of this position and access. The temptation to tamper, to distort, or to falsify records and data to serve a dishonest motive for selfish gain can easily gain a foothold for these people if they are not careful.

Merriam-Webster's Dictionary defines tampering as follows: "to carry on underhand negotiations (as by bribery); to interfere so as to weaken or change." We can express this another way by saying that tampering available records will help a person make something bad appear good to suit his purposes. This is done to lead clients and people to trust the agency or the corporation and the people in charge of running it. But the Bible says, "Woe to those who call evil good, and good evil; who put darkness for light, and light for darkness; who put bitter for sweet, and sweet for bitter! Woe to those who are wise in their own eyes, and prudent in their own sight" (Isa. 5:20–21).

Sometimes another trusted party is involved in the tampering or distortion of facts, data, or a report in connivance with the officers or officials of a particular business sector in order to make it appear that everything about the business operation is doing well. The auditor, whether in the public sector or the private sector, has an important role to play to prevent tampering.

In the public sector, a change in government administration usually brings with it a change in the officials responsible for the audit of expenditures against the allocations of its budget. This case will create a very sensitive situation for the auditors who are appointed and will be beholden to the administrative powers who appointed them.

On the other hand, in the private sector, where the auditing function is provided by outside independent entities, there is need for ethically independent auditors to be honest and concerned with the interest of the corporation's creditors, stockholders, and the public as a safety check against corrupt practices.

Nepotism

Nepotism is known as favoritism shown to a relative, most often in the granting of jobs.[12] It usually demoralizes rank-and-file employees in the public sector where employee job selection is governed by civil service rules. This practice corrupts the moral fiber of a public organization.

Cronyism

Cronyism is what happens when a person of authority appoints good friends to important positions under his supervision without regard to their competence or qualifications. Usually the appointing person feels inadequate in his job and appoints someone he feels he can trust and who will not to come against him and his views.

Governments are more likely accused of this practice because they use tax money paid by the people in their operations: "It is not unusual for a politician to surround him- or herself with highly-qualified subordinates, and to develop social, business, or political friendships leading to the appointment to office of friends, likewise in granting government contracts. In fact, the counsel of such friends is why the officeholder successfully obtained his or her powerful position."[13] Appointing these friends to a position is a way of acknowledging their help.

Cronyism in the private sector is sometimes called the "old boys' club" or "the golden circle." Cronyism in this sector also involves mutual connections and interactions of influential people in the conduct of their businesses. This is what is called "crony capitalism," which is against the standards of good business practice. The Enron fraud is an extreme example of crony capitalism.[14]

A high official in government has the right to appoint people he knows and trusts to sensitive positions because he is given the authority to appoint. However, cronyism results in inefficiency, and also results in confusion about the responsibilities, duties, control, or management of processes to be done. This has the tendency to erode the confidence of people in the established authority and rule of law.

Mr. Randy David, in a column titled "No Place for Buddies" in the *Philippine Daily Inquirer*, wrote that appointments made to sensitive government positions "reveals how…the personal tends to be dysfunctionally woven into the institutional, resulting in many of the recurrent government problems" they encounter.[15]

Mr. David wrote further: "Government service is a demanding vocation. When one becomes a public servant, his first loyalty has to be to the nation, not to the person who appointed him.... We can be good public servants and faithful friends at the same time—but to do this, we have to keep these two roles as far away from one another as possible.... In short, the bottom line is that friends have to be qualified for the jobs to which they are appointed, especially if these are very important positions."[16]

INSIDER TRADING

The United States Securities and Exchange Commission (SEC) classifies insider trading in two forms: the legal and the illegal.[17] Insider trading is considered legal when insiders in a corporation—officers, directors, and employees—trade stocks in the company and report such transactions to the SEC in accordance with the legal framework of such transactions. Illegal insider trading, on the other hand, "refers generally to buying or selling a security, in breach of fiduciary duty or other relationship of trust and confidence, while in possession of material, nonpublic information about the security. Insider trading violations may also include 'tipping' such information, securities trading by the person 'tipped,' and securities trading by those who misappropriate such information."[18]

Insider trading involves activities related to the buying or selling of securities (investments) of a corporation in accordance with established rules and regulations.

It becomes illegal and immoral when those who have knowledge of or access to information not yet known to the public take advantage of that knowledge to use it for their own advantage, or the advantage of others, in the trading of securities affected by such knowledge. The intent is to take advantage of information not yet known to the public or the investors for selfish gain and the protection of personal interest.

UNLAWFUL
MONETARY TRANSACTIONS

On August 15, 2010, Yahoo News Canada published a report from Washington (AFP), which quoted a report from the *Wall Street Journal* about "an Apple employee [who] has been charged with selling secrets to Asian suppliers of the tech giant in exchange for at least one million dollars in kickbacks."[19]

There are many ways of transacting money unlawfully and they are evolving and adapting to the times and seasons. The love of money drives these illegal monetary transactions to flourish. The shrewd can gain money illegally through unlawful activities or by trading banned, or even good, commodities against laws and good morals. Traders of illegal stuff, of humans, even of non-existent things, have used evolving schemes designed to deceive and defraud the unsuspecting, as knowledge increases as prophesied in the Bible. (See Daniel 12:4, 10.)

Suppression of Data

Electronic suppression of data is similar to manipulation except that a machine is employed to do the work electronically to suppress cash sales data.

A report by the Canadian Press told of the two-year pilot project of the Canada Revenue Services that started in 2008 to probe selected restaurants suspected of electronic suppression of sales (ESS) in the conduct of their business. The ESS is done through "phantom-ware . . . software within electronic cash registers that can selectively delete sales records leaving no audit trail."[20] This activity defrauds the government of tax payments it is supposed to earn from these businesses. Millions of dollars suppressed from cash sales was uncovered in this particular case.

The above ways of corruption are easily noticed by people because it occurs in the midst of society. People corporately experience the impact of their effects. However, the octopus Satan is a deceiver and a silent worker. He also waits silently, ready to attack individually those he can devour as you will read in the following chapter.

Chapter 6

OTHER WAYS
OF CORRUPTION

As we've already explored, Adam disobeyed
God's command not to eat of the tree of the
knowledge of good and evil, and as a result of
his sin, the image of God in Adam was corrupted. His sin
of disobedience resulted a new corruptible state of being.
As a consequence of Adam's sin, his descendants also
inherited this corruptible nature and gained the tendency
to be corrupted. This means Adam was separated from the
grace of God, and so are you and I.

Merriam-Webster's Dictionary defines sin as "an offense
especially against God; a weakened state of human nature
in which the self is estranged from God." From this

definition, you may conclude that every offense against God is sin.

King Solomon, the wisest king who ever lived, said, "For there is not a just man on earth who does good and does not sin" (Eccl. 7:20). Also, if we say that we have no sin, we deceive ourselves (1 John 1:8). Sin is an offense against God. God is a holy God, and He desires you to be holy (1 Pet. 1:16). God is righteous in all His ways, and He desires your obedience to His commands, just as He desired Adam's obedience in the beginning.

Sin is the catalyst that starts corruption, and sin fuels corruption.

In the preceding chapter, you read about the most visible works of corruption in the world, yet there are other things against the righteous will of God that are silently happening in your midst. In this chapter, we'll explore those hidden forms of corruption.

CORRUPTION
OF HUMAN LIFE

The world cries out loud in protest and condemnation when innocent lives are murdered mercilessly in homes, in daycare centers, in schools, in the streets, and in places of war and conflict. But you hear only a stifled cry that slowly dies for the multitude of innocent and helpless lives cut off prematurely before they ever see the light of day.

Although happening silently and unnoticed by many, a glaring example of corruption of human life is abortion.

The U.S. Supreme Court ruled favorably in 1973 on the lower court's decision regarding *Roe v. Wade* that a Texas law criminalizing abortion is against a woman's right of privacy in the constitution. This case started in 1970 when "Jane Roe" (actually Norma McCorvey) brought action against the State of Texas, represented by Henry Wade, district attorney of Dallas county.[1]

In her book *Life in the Matrix*, Karen Blanks Adams wrote about the deception caused by this landmark case that legalized abortion in the United States. She wrote that three decades after the Supreme Court's decision, "Ms. McCorvey petitioned the U.S. District Court for the Northern District of Texas, Dallas Division (where the case was first heard) to reopen the original Roe v. Wade case in light of new evidence that was not available in 1973."[2] Ms. McCorvey submitted an affidavit to present evidence that hadn't been included in her earlier case. She made the petition in the hope of seeking to end "the tragedy that arose from [her] unsuspecting acquiescence in allowing [her life] to be used to legalize abortion."[3]

Among the statements that Ms. McCorvey swore in her affidavit, we learn that Ms. McCorvey claimed the earlier decision for *Roe v. Wade* was based on false assumptions. She said, "Because the courts allowed my case to proceed without my testimony, without ever explaining to me the reality of abortion, without being cross-examined on my erroneous perception of abortion, a tragic mistake was made."[4] Through this affidavit, Ms. McCorvey attempted to reverse the decision that had been originally made in *Roe v. Wade*.

We learn from the affidavit that Ms. McCorvey was never given any information about the case or the reality of abortion:

> As the class action plaintiff in the most controversial U.S. Supreme Court case of the twentieth century, I only met with the attorneys twice. Once over pizza and beer, when I was told that my baby was only "tissue" and another time at Coffee's office to sign the affidavit. I had no other personal contacts. I was never invited into court. I never testified. I was never present before any court on any level, and I was never at any hearing on my case. The entire case was an *abstraction*. The facts about abortion were never heard. Totally excluded from every aspect and every issue of the case, I found out about the decision from the newspaper just like the rest of the country.[5]

What's more, Ms McCorvey never had the abortion on which the *Roe v. Wade* case was based—in fact, she gave the baby up for adoption. In the succeeding years of her life, she had difficulty finding a job, but because of "Roe" she was able to work in abortion clinics. Her years of work in that environment eventually caused her to give up this kind of work and become an advocate against abortion. This is when she petitioned the courts to reconsider its ruling on *Roe v. Wade*.

Unfortunately, the district court ruled against McCorvey's affidavit in 2003, holding that "McCorvey's thirty-year delay is of such a great magnitude that her motion was not made within a reasonable time due to the length of time alone."[6] The district court denied McCorvey's motion for relief from judgement.

It is worthy to quote the following statements from the fifth circuit court's decision that reflect the judge's struggle as she wrote the decision:

> The perverse result of the court's ruling having determined through *constitutional adjudication* this fundamental policy, which affects over a million women and unborn babies each year, *is that the facts no longer matter.* This is a peculiar outcome for a Court so committed to "life" that it struggles with the particular facts of dozens of death penalty cases each year.... Hard and social science will of course progress even though the Supreme Court averts its eyes. It takes no expert prognosticator to know that research on women's mental and physical health following abortion will yield an eventual medical consensus, and neonatal

science will push the frontiers of fetal "visibility" ever closer to the date of conception. One may fervently hope that the court will someday acknowledge such developments and reevaluate Roe and Casey accordingly.[7]

The court said "*the facts no longer matter.*" But God says, "Come now, and let us reason together...though your sins are like scarlet, they shall be as white as snow; though they are red like crimson, they shall be as wool" (Isa. 1:18). Jesus says, "Not one of the sparrows sold in the market falls to the ground apart from the Father's will, and you are of more value than many sparrows" (Matt. 10:29, 31, author's paraphrase).

As Satan intruded into the sinless existence of Adam and Eve in the presence of God in Eden, he now intrudes anywhere and upon anyone to come against God's righteousness. King Solomon, in the Book of Ecclesiastes, wrote, "Moreover I saw under the sun: in the place of judgment, wickedness was there; and in the place of righteousness, iniquity was there.... Then I returned and considered all the oppression that is done under the sun: and look! The tears of the oppressed, but they have no comforter—on the side of their oppressors there is power, but they have no comforter" (Eccl. 3:16; 4:1).

It is indeed painful and sad to think that Satan's deception has resulted in many helpless unborn human beings for more than three decades—all because Satan used a good thing, a woman's fundamental "right of privacy," as the reason. And after those years, more helpless innocent lives are still being lost because of Satan's continuing deception, this time through the use of another good thing: the exercise of law built on the premise of righteousness. The corruption of unborn human life is silently happening, and the blood of the unborn babies is crying out for redemption from the ground.

The Lord formed their inward part; they are covered in their mothers' wombs. They are fearfully and wonderfully made; they are the Lord's marvelous works. Their frames were not hidden from Him when they were made in secret and skillfully wrought in the lowest parts of the earth. The Lord saw their substance being yet unformed—and in His book, they all were written, their days, when as yet there were none of them. (See Psalm 139.)

Yet the lives of these helpless unborn humans are cut off prematurely, and this is outside the will of God. Corruption prevents these beings from living the life God purposed for each one of them.

We give thanks that even though "all unrighteousness is sin" (1 John 5:17), there is no unrighteousness with God, for He says, "I will have mercy on whomever I will have mercy, and I will have compassion on whomever I will have compassion" (Rom. 9:15). Jesus also says, "Come to Me, all you who labor and are heavy laden, and I will give you rest. Take My yoke upon you and learn from Me, for I am gentle and lowly in heart, and you will find rest for your souls" (Matt. 11:28–29). Additionally, God says, "I will forgive you…your sins I will remember no more (Jer. 31:34, author's paraphrase). Those who have suffered from the corruption of abortion will find forgiveness, compassion, mercy, and rest in God.

CORRUPTION OF TRUTH

Terry Law and Jim Gilbert wrote in their book *The Hope Habit*, "If you read the newspaper, watch television, browse the Internet, or attend a secular school, then truth is under siege."[8] What is fed into your homes, they said, "tries to control both what you see and how you interpret it, filtering everything through the lens of political correctness…. They either twist the facts or ignore them altogether."[9] Thus, your home is bombarded with corrupted truths.

The apostle Peter wrote, "And many will follow their destructive ways, because of whom the way of truth will be blasphemed. By covetousness they will exploit you with deceptive words" (2 Pet. 2:2–3). The book of Romans says, "The wrath of God is revealed from heaven against all ungodliness and unrighteousness of men, who suppress the truth in unrighteousness" (Rom. 1:18). Again, the Bible admonishes us, "Let no corrupt word proceed out of your

mouth, but what is good for necessary moral enlighten-
ment of the hearers" (Ephesians 4:29, author's paraphrase).

Corruption of Morals and Ways of Living

In *The Hope Habit*, Law and Gilbert also wrote: "Above all,
traditional Biblical ethics have been abandoned in favor of
either legitimizing sinful behavior as personal 'preference'
or excusing it as disease. On the one hand, perversion is
declared normal, and on the other, bad results are 'not
your fault.'"[10]

Your ways are always before the Lord. Although your
ways may seem right for you, as they always do before a
man, their end is the way of death. If the way is broad and
easy, it leads to corruption. Without the fear of God in
our hearts, it is easy for us to fall in into this way of corruptive living. (See Proverbs 5:21; 14:12; Matthew 7:13; and
Romans 3:17.)

Corruption of Sports

The sports world is also affected by corruption. As one
example, a report in the *New York Times* on August 30,
2010, told of a cricket-fixing scandal in Pakistan concerning the fourth test-match game between Pakistan and
England. In this form of corruption in the sports world,

"instead of bribing players to fix matches outright...the schemes often rely on fixing details of play that—while not necessarily affecting a game's outcome—can attract millions of dollars of bets."[11]

CONCLUSION

In all of these methods of corruption discussed here and the previous chapter, the main motive is to hide all illegal and immoral activities from being seen and discovered by others. Both the corruptor and the corrupted think that by hiding their activities they will be safe. This is the way of corruption.

Satan operates in men whose hearts are darkened by sin. He also operates through deceit and lies. He can make something sinful appear so pleasing—something disdainful appear desirable—in order to deceive the unsuspecting. In this way, those who are driven and taken hold of by the Corruptor are totally sold out in believing that carefully hiding their unrighteous ways keeps them safe and free from receiving what they deserve from the law for their unrighteousness. They are totally unaware that their ways are not hidden from God, who sees everything they are doing whether good or bad (Prov. 5:21). They follow with zest their earthly and corrupt ways that bring the curse on the head of the poor. They pervert the way of the righteous. But God, who is the light of man, will bring every hidden work into the light. Even the darkness of your life is not beyond the expanse of His light (Ps. 139:11–12).

Chapter 7

UNMASKING
THE CORRUPTOR

MY FATHER DIED when I was five. After he died, my mother and us, her children, lived with my maternal grandparents. My grandfather was a pastor, a farmer, a fisherman, and a carpenter—all in one. Being a pastor was his calling, and the rest were his occupations—the sources of our livelihood.

My grandfather's way of relaxing after a day's work was to read his Bible while I played at his feet. He would read his Bible aloud, although there was no one else around to hear but me. What I didn't know then was that he was sowing the Word of God in my spirit.

I would also hear him explain how the five senses of man—sight, hearing, taste, feeling, and smell, which make up man's soul—were given by God for man to use for his own good. These words I heard from my grandfather as a child still stand in my mind even after so many years.

As a poor orphan, I was shy and quiet in the company of other kids in school. They wore nice clothes and shoes. They had money for snacks, while I had a sandwich my mother had prepared for me. Everytime I looked at those kids, I felt so little, so inferior. I had no friends at that age.

One day in school, I saw a penny fall on the ground that a girl dropped. It rolled and stopped right in front of me. The girl didn't notice.

Suddenly, I felt a struggle deep inside me. I wrestled between the thought of getting the penny for myself or telling the girl her money had dropped on the floor. I had never touched money up to that point in my life. I struggled with the temptation to take it. I was feeling covetous; getting the coin that wasn't mine was so strong in my mind.

I gingerly placed my foot over the coin to hide it under my slipper, and I figured out how to pick it up later from the floor when nobody was looking. But after a while, the fear of taking what was not mine got hold of me. I knew it was wrong. I slowly removed my foot from the coin and called the attention of the girl, and she happily picked up her money.

The fear of God, planted by Holy Spirit and sustained through the words read to me by my grandfather from the

Bible, overpowered the temptation that urged me to get the penny that was not mine. I thought God would not be pleased with me if I stole that money. It was wrong, and God hates what is wrong.

So I did not get the penny. But God did give me a friend. That girl became my very first friend. After that incident, she always gave me a flower from her garden every school day.

This memory has been with me for many years. The beautiful flowers still pictured in my mind are reminders of God's wonderful power to deliver and to save those who fear Him (Jer. 15:21). The fear of God that my grandfather patiently planted in my heart by reading God's Word preserved me from committing the sin of covetousness. I feared the Lord and did not follow the evil thought in my mind (Prov. 3:7).

This was my first lesson in making the right decision between two choices. The fear of the Lord gave me wisdom to do the right thing and made me understand the consequence if I did otherwise (Ps. 111:10).As I look back, I believe God's angels were with me that day and actually moved my foot away from the penny. The Bible says that angels are ministering spirits sent forth by God to minister to those who are to inherit salvation (Heb. 1:14). God's angels prevented me from taking that money which was not mine and kept me from committing the sin of covetousness.

What happened may seem normal for children my age, and people may shrug their shoulders, laugh it off, and forget all about it. I was only a young child then. I was at that age others may call the age of innocence. But had I given in to the temptation to take the penny, it would have been the beginning of sin in my life. The sins would have grown bigger and bigger. It would have been the start of my life of corruption. The book of James says, "But each one is tempted when he is drawn away by his own desires and enticed. Then, when desire had conceived, it gives birth to sin; and sin, when it is full-grown, brings forth death. Do not be deceived my beloved brethren" (James 1:14–16).

Through the years, I have wondered why I placed my foot over the penny. Why did I act that way? As I became more acquainted with the Scriptures, I realized I was born a sinner, just like everyone else (Ps. 51:5).

Satan's sole purpose consists of doing everything against the purposes of God. His abode is in the atmosphere. He is the prince of the power of the air, the spirit who now works in the sons of disobedience (Eph. 2:2). He roams the earth and is the king of this world. He is out to seek the destruction of man and of your life.

But God's purpose for you is always for good—to glorify Him. It follows that because Satan coveted God's glory, he will hate everything that glorifies God. The apostle Peter reminded us, then, "Be sober, be vigilant; because your adversary the devil walks about like a roaring lion, seeking whom he may devour" (1 Pet. 5:8). Satan wants to catch as prey people he can enslave to corruption and destroy. As he rebelled against God, he is at every opportunity coming against you to capture you to serve his evil purposes and prevent the good plan of God for you. He covets even that glory for himself.

Satan coveted God's glory and rebelled against Him in heaven. Consequently, he was thrown out of heaven to the earth, but only until God's determined time of judgment. The time will come when God is going to render the final judgment on Satan, his demons, and the unrepentant. In the meantime, Satan continues to oppose every move of God and everything God has planned for His creation—especially God's good plan for you.

Jesus said, "The thief [Satan] does not come except to steal, and to kill, and to destroy. I have come that you may have life, and that you may have it more abundantly" (John 10:10). God has a better purpose for you. He sent His Son Jesus, the Son of God and the Son of Man, to save you from Satan's schemes. God demonstrates His own love for us, in that while we were still sinners, Christ died for us (Rom. 5:8). He finished and perfected what you cannot do to save yourself from death. He offered Himself as a perfect sacrifice, beaten and nailed to the cross for your corruption (Isa. 53:5).

Jesus offered Himself for you and me. Your infirmities and iniquities were laid upon Jesus and nailed on the palms of His hands; your sinful ways were nailed on His feet on the cross (Ps. 22:16). He gave out His last breath and finished the work of redemption for you and for me by shedding His blood and the water in it.

By Jesus' offering of His body and blood, He erased the curse of death for you. By the blood of Jesus, you have been redeemed from the hand of Satan (1 Pet. 1:18–19). Jesus did everything once and for all to save from spiritual death those who will trust Him. This is the way Father provided to bring you back to His image.

Jesus "is the propitiation for our sins, and not for ours only but also for the whole world" (1 John 2:2). There is nothing else you can do but acknowledge that Jesus finished His redemptive work for you at the cross—believe it, and appropriate it for yourself:

> Knowing this, that our old man was crucified with Him, that the body of sin might be done away with, that we should no longer be slaves of sin."
>
> —ROMANS 6:6

Corruption creeps into our lives in seemingly harmless ways. The Corruptor starts by deceiving his intended victim, just as Satan did by hiding in the body of the serpent to deceive Eve. He uses deceptive tactics to lead you to rethink your moral principles. While you are reflecting on the pros and cons of your moral principles, he will offer things that will cause you to be tempted to do his unrighteous will.

The baits offered by the Corruptor will always cater to the needs and cravings of your sinful nature. These three reactions of the flesh—lust of the eyes, lust of the flesh, and pride—led Eve to desire the forbidden fruit. The fruit looked pleasant to her eyes. It was so tempting. She craved to eat it; and more, it would make her like God knowing the good from the evil. This thought led her to desire it more. This is the same manner employed by Satan to tempt you to fall into his corruptive schemes.

Corruption begins when someone is tempted to desire to do something wrong, or to have something good but get it in the wrong way or at the wrong time. To let anything that is wrong have its way and do nothing to prevent it makes it easier for Satan to snatch you into his corruptive scheme.

Desire is temptation conceived. Sin is temptation birthed. No one is exempt from temptation, for we live in a fallen world where Satan seeks complete rule. Satan will always look for his victims. The apostle Paul admonished us "to be sober, to be vigilant; because your adversary the devil walks about like a roaring lion, seeking whom he may devour. Resist him steadfast in the faith" (1 Pet. 5:8). Satan is a predator and the Corruptor, the author and master of corruption.

Jesus took Peter and the two sons of Zebedee with him

to Gethsemane and told them to stay in a certain spot in the garden and watch with Him while He prayed in a spot a little farther away from them. But when He returned, they were sleeping. He reprimanded the disciples and told them, "What? Could you not watch with Me one hour?" (Matt. 26:40). The disciples knew the Lord, and they were known to Jesus. They were with Him since the start of His earthly ministry. They were with the Son of God made flesh as the Son of Man. But they failed to watch with the Lord; they fell asleep.

We are just like these three disciples. You may have known the Lord. You may have surrendered to Jesus as the Master of your life. But then you are overwhelmed with everything you are facing. You are tired and bored of the place you are right now. You are tired of praying; tired of waiting; tired of hoping for the answer to your prayers. You feel weak. You are ready to give up hope. But the Lord says to you, "Watch and pray, lest you enter into temptation. The spirit indeed is willing, but the flesh is weak" (v. 41). Jesus likes you not to lose faith in His power to help you and intervene in your situation. Prayer and the Word will protect you from being tempted.

The person involved in corruption tends to savor all the pleasures and worldly fulfillment, gratification of the flesh, and self-esteem offered by the Corruptor until he is almost at the brink of no return. Satan, in his inherent wickedness, fuels your desire for more and more of the wages of corruption. Once you fall into the devil's trap of corruption and are unrepentant, you will become a servant to it and a slave to Satan's wicked schemes. Satan will tempt you to do more corrupt things over and over again until you have no peace, your life is broken, and your future seems so unsure. God says, "As I live, I have no pleasure in the death of the wicked, but that the wicked turn from his evil way and live" (Ezek. 33:11). God is not willing that any should die spiritually but that all should come to repentance (2 Pet. 3:9), for if you live according to the flesh, you will die a spiritual death, but if you live by the Spirit, you will put to death the deeds of the body and have eternal life (Rom. 8:13).

Satan succeeded in making Eve doubt the word of God. In doubting God's word, she ate of the fruit of the forbidden tree. She was deceived "and fell into transgression" (1 Tim. 2:14). She gave the fruit from the forbidden tree to Adam, who also ate it. Adam disobeyed God and sinned willfully, and Satan thought he had succeeded in his plan to prevent God's purpose of creating man for His glory.

But the Lord of hosts says, "I have purposed, and who will annul it? My hand is stretched out, and who will turn it back?" (Isa. 14:27, author's paraphrase). The Triune God created man in His image so you could give Him glory. His purpose stands. No one can reverse it. It will come to pass.

Chapter 8

HIDING BEHIND CORRUPTION

A FEW YEARS AGO, I experienced my first time driving during a heavy snowfall. I was on my way to buy medicine for my sick daughter-in-law when the snow started to fall. I would have not gone out to drive in that kind of weather except for this urgent reason, and nobody was at home who could buy the medicine for her.

So I took her car and drove to the drugstore. Visibility was bad. While I waited to make a left turn into the drugstore, the car in front of me turned left. I thought it was safe to go, and I followed that car. I forgot my driving lessons. I did not check to see if it was safe to make a left turn, but I did it anyway. Slowly, I steered the car, and then *bam!* A small truck hit the right front corner of the car. Thankfully, God protected me. I was not hurt, but the car was damaged. It had to be fixed so it could be used again. My daughter-in-law's insurance company covered the cost of repairs to put the car back into working order.

This relates to what happens between us and God.

To review, Satan knew Adam was created from dust, which crumbles. So Satan hid in the serpent's body to confuse and deceive Eve, Adam's wife. He lied to her, telling her she would not die if she ate the fruit of the forbidden tree. Eve was deceived and ate of the fruit, and she brought one to Adam. Adam did not think twice. He forgot God's command and was encouraged—Eve's face showed delight, and she was still alive! So Adam also ate the fruit.

In Adam's eyes, Eve must have looked just fine after eating the fruit. In fact, nothing had happened to her physically, as far as he could observe with his eyes. He might have thought the fruit must have been good to eat. So Adam decided to follow what Eve had done. He forgot what God had commanded him.

Adam's godly DNA was tweaked by the entrance of the sin of disobedience into his life. By his sin, Adam's gene was also tweaked and infused with the corrupted nature of Satan. Adam's godly nature was permeated by sin, by which he received its wages: death (Rom. 6:23). Thereby all of Adam's descendants, you and I, have fallen from the grace of God. We have inherited Adam's tweaked gene and become a fallen race.

So you have two natures in yourself: the godly image of God and the sinful nature of Adam. These two natures are contrary to each other and continue to war inside of you. Your sinful nature always would like to dominate your life's decisions and actions. But be careful: "Do you not know that to whom you present yourselves to obey, you are that one's slaves whom you obey, whether of sin leading to death, or of obedience leading to righteousness?" (Rom. 6:16). There is warfare going on inside of you. For "the flesh lusts against the Spirit, and the Spirit against the flesh; and these are contrary to one another, so that you do not do the things that you wish" (Gal. 5:17). If you obey your flesh, you will reap corruption, but if you sow to the Spirit, you will reap everlasting life (Gal. 6:8).

But God wants to restore fallen and sinful man to Himself. His Spirit tries to revive your godly nature back into the fullness of the image of God which He created you to be. The godly image of God in you gives you the ability to receive God's grace, the gift of life in Jesus Christ.

God is a good God (Ps. 25:8). He is a wise God (Rom. 16:27). After the fall of Adam, He provided a plan and a way to fix man back into the godly image He had originally created him to have. God provided insurance to fix sinful man back to the fullness of His original godly nature in God's image. God so loved you that He gave His Son, Jesus, perfect Man and perfect God, to atone for your sins. Before His crucifixion, Jesus said to Thomas, the doubting disciple, "I am the way, the truth, and the life. No one comes to the Father except through Me" (John 14:6).

In Jesus, you can have your life retrieved back from the pit of corruption where it is heading and out of the curse of death that you have inherited from the generational curse of sin since Adam. Jesus' sacrifice on the cross is God's perfect insurance for you to reform youself back into His image that He had planned for you, for "Christ was offered once to bear the sins of many" (Heb. 9:28). He has reconciled you to God by carrying on His own sinless body your infirmities and iniquities—through His death—to present you holy and blameless before God (Col. 1:21–22).

Jesus' blood was the ransom paid for the price of your sin, even for the sins of all men in the whole world. You were redeemed "with the precious blood of Christ as of a lamb without blemish and without spot" (1 Pet. 1:19) from your aimless conduct that you did all your life. And God completely sealed Jesus' sacrifice on the cross to bring you back to Him with His Holy Spirit.

Like the damaged car, you can be restored back to God.

As my late grandfather explained it, God created man with five senses for him to use for his own good. These are: the sense of sight, the sense of taste, the sense of smell, the sense of hearing, and the sense of feeling. We use these five senses to interact with our environment.

THE TEMPTATION OF JESUS IN THE WILDERNESS

The book of Matthew tells the story of Jesus, the Son of Man, being tempted by Satan in the wilderness. Jesus was hungry, having fasted forty days and forty nights, and the tactics Satan used attempted to arouse the five senses of the Son of Man: the senses of feeling, sight, taste, smell, and hearing.

First, the devil tried to arouse the need of Jesus' flesh for food. He tempted Jesus to command the stone to become bread. But Jesus answered Satan, saying, "It is written, 'Man shall not live by bread alone, but by every word that proceeds from the mouth of God'" (Matt. 4:3–4).

Then the devil tried to arouse pride in Jesus. He took Him "up into the pinnacle of the temple" in the holy city and said to Him, "If You are the Son of God, throw Yourself down. For it is written: 'He shall give His angels charge over you,' and, 'in their hands they shall bear you up, lest you dash your foot against a stone.'" But Jesus said to him, "It is written again, 'You shall not tempt the Lord your God'" (vv. 5–7).

Again, the devil took Jesus up on an exceedingly high

mountain and showed Him all the kingdoms of the world and their glory. And he said to Him, "All these things I will give You if You will fall down and worship me" (vv. 8–9). In this, the devil tried to arouse the lust of the eyes in Jesus.

But Jesus resisted all these temptations. He said, "Away with you, Satan! For it is written, 'You shall worship the LORD your God and Him only you shall serve.' Then the devil left Him, and behold, angels came and ministered to Him" (vv. 10–11).

No servant is greater than his master (John 13:16). If the devil tempted Jesus, how much more will he tempt you also. Therefore, be careful not to think you are standing strong, lest you fall into temptation (1 Cor. 10:12). The tactics employed by Satan are very subtle. All his devices to entrap you will try to stimulate your five senses to arouse the lust of your eyes, the lust of your flesh, and the pride of your life. The devil will attack you in an area of your life where you are weak at a time when you are most vulnerable to temptation.

Just as God sees you all the time and knows everything about you, even the contents of your heart and mind and the words you are going to say even before you utter them (Heb. 4:13; Ps. 139:4), Satan observes you also. Remember, he is always searching for victims to trap into corruption. He hears your words and your conversations, except that he cannot read your mind. He is observing any particular thing you are doing and any particular word you are saying that he can use as his point of entry to tempt you. Be careful of what you say, then, and "guard your mouth and tongue to keep your soul from troubles" (Prov. 21:23). Jesus also said, "Watch and pray, lest you enter into temptation. The spirit indeed is willing, but the flesh is weak" (Matt. 26:41).

Corruption is a state of rottenness born out of sin and fueled by sin. Having committed the first sin in the universe, Satan is the real "being" hiding behind corruption.

KNOW YOUR ENEMY

In military warfare, if you know the enemy, his character, and his behavior, you already have an advantage over him to win the battle. In medicine, doctors can treat and administer the right medication and can manage correctly any medical condition when the virus, microbe, or cause of the sickness is identified. Likewise, you need to know who is behind corruption in order to win in your fight against it.

We've already determined that Satan is the source behind all corruption in the world. To better understand the nature, characteristics, and behavior of the Corruptor, then, we compared him with an octopus in chapter three. He is intrusive and proud. He is a predator that is always looking for a prey, just like the octopus, to feed its growth.

He also wants to enlarge his army of the corrupted to gain control of the whole world. He is the power, like the main brain of the octopus, and he gives orders to his demons, which are like the tentacles, to draw men to corruption and enslave them.

Satan is malignant like cancer, drawing men to destruction and death. He desires that you give your life in exchange for the things of this world (Job 2:4). Like the octopus, he is cunning, able, and very knowledgeable in the methods he uses. He deceives his victims with his tricks and abilities and even presents himself harmless and as one of your kind. He can even "transform himself into an angel of light" (2 Cor. 11:14). He is fierce and wicked, like the octopus, hunting for helpless victims to consume. Satan "was a murderer" and "a liar and the father of lies" (John 8:44).

When your senses are stirred to lust after something, temptation can easily penetrate your sinful nature to desire that thing. When you are tempted and your desire awakens and you give in to your desires, then you commit sin. This is how corruption attaches itself into the hearts and the lives of people. It creeps so subtly, hardly noticeable. You will not know it has begun until you are already caught in its tide.

Corruption is infectious and cancerous. It is a social disease and is hard to conquer. It is sleazy as a snake. The moment you say, "I will," to that which is against the will of God, the corrupting process begins in your life. Everything against the will of God is sin. The Corruptor, Satan, never stops in his work to corrupt as many people as he can, as he continues to war against the Almighty God and His good plan for man. And he always seeks out man, who was created in the image of God, as his victim.

But Satan's time is short, for he and his demons will be judged by God (Isa. 14:15; Jude 6; Rev. 20:10). He will always try to establish as much corruption as he can in the earth and corrupt as many victims as he can because he knows his time is short and he will be judged.

So, then, in the fight against corruption, you "do not wrestle against flesh and blood but against principalities, against powers, against the rulers of the darkness of this age, against spiritual hosts of wickedness in the heavenly places" (Eph. 6:12). Yes, there are people in the world that the devil has captured to be agents (corruptors) and workers (corrupted) in his corrupt schemes. But your real enemy is Satan and the hosts of his demons working with him.

Are you in a place where it seems the air is very thin because the seeds of corruption planted by the Corruptor have grown and are starting to bear bad fruit? Are you at a point where everything seems hopeless because hope is sucked out by the evils of corruption? Are you at the point of giving up and joining the band.

You may think you cannot do anything to fight against and defeat corruption. No way. I think we all are in one or more of these situations. The world and its system where we live continue to spin into the fullness of corruption. We are constantly observing corruption in the public sector, in the private sector, in the marketplace, in the home, in religion, in morals, and in every other area of the world. Satan is the god of the world system. He is the prince of the powers of the air. He uses everything within his means to bombard institutions, homes, and families. He uses you and me with his lies and deceitful ways. His intention is to corrupt as many people as he can to prevent you from attaining God's good purpose for you.

Take heart! God is still seated on His throne in heaven. His throne is forever and ever; a scepter of righteousness is the scepter of His kingdom (Heb. 1:8). "God shall sit and rule on His throne" (Zech. 6:13). To him who overcomes being corrupted God will grant to sit with Him on His throne, as Christ has also overcome and sat down with the Father on His throne. (See Revelation 3:21.)

Chapter 9

HOW CORRUPTION
CONTROLS THE WORLD

E LIVE IN a time of turmoil, suffering, strife, poverty, and uncertainty, a time when "evil men and impostors will grow worse and worse, deceiving and being deceived" (2 Tim. 3:13). In our time and age, corruption is prevalent and occurring almost everywhere. Satan is the god of the world system. He will choose any place where there are people whose hearts can easily be deceived and fall easily to temptation and believe the lies of the evil one. The heart of man is deceitful above all things, and desperately wicked (Jer. 17:9). Satan knows the right time to strike his victims. He will choose anyone, even the unsuspecting ones who trust in their own righteousness and strength, to implement his agenda of corruption. His ultimate motive is to prevent the glory of God from filling the whole earth (Ps. 148) and for God's glory not to shine upon His people (Isa. 60:2).

The Lord says:

> Let not the wise man glory in his wisdom, let not the mighty man glory in his might, nor let the rich man glory in his riches; but let him who glories glory in this, that he understands and knows Me, that I am the Lord, exercising lovingkindness, judgment, and righteousness in the earth, for in these I delight.
>
> —JEREMIAH 9:23–24

Because of his fallen nature, man easily succumbs to temptation and commits sin. Our vulnerability to temptation is further aggravated by many factors: the modern world and advances in communication, ignorance of what is right and what is wrong, belief systems, and traditions. We live in a world where people get used to believing and doing those things that they see others are doing or believing. The self in man wills; it is very strong. The self usually reigns in your heart, and the knowledge of the true God, if there is any at all, stays only in your head. The fear of people and what they will say is stronger than the fear of God and what God says. Pleasing people is natural for you and me.

Man is always self-confident: "A wise man fears and

departs from evil but a fool rages in his heart" (Prov. 14:16). Man is also hard-headed, as the Lord, speaking through Isaiah, said, "I have spoken to you but you have not heard, and I have called to you but you have not answered" (Isa. 65:12, author's paraphrase).

But God says, "I, the Lord, speak righteousness, I declare things that are right" (Isa. 45:19) and "Why, when I called, there was none to answer?" (Isa. 50:2). Could the Lord be speaking the same words to you today?

Man seeks his own good and always wants to be self-sufficient. The apostle Paul wrote to the Philippian Christians: "For all seek their own, not the things which are of Christ Jesus" (Phil. 2:21). Man by nature is undeniably selfish. This is the effect of Satan's selfishness imputed upon Adam and passed on to his descendants—you and me. The prophet Isaiah, wrote, "Yes, they are greedy dogs which never have enough. And they are shepherds who cannot understand; they all look to their own way, everyone for his own gain, from his own territory" (Isa. 56:11).

When Adam sinned in the garden of Eden, his "corruptible DNA was passed on to their children and to every generations following since then."[1] Adam and Eve were banished from Eden, out of a life of ease and abundance into a difficult life in their new corruptible environment. Man began to toil for his needs in order to eat outside the garden of Eden, where weeds and thistles competed for the nutrients of the soil (Gen. 3:17–19).

Because you had inherited Adam's tweaked gene in his corrupted DNA, as well as his need to work for survival, you are even more of a vulnerable pawn for Satan's corruptive schemes. You, and everyone else, are likely prey for his purpose.

It is easy to fall into and accept any concept presented to you if you do not understand the principle behind the concept. As the Bible says, "People are destroyed for lack of knowledge" (Hos. 4:6). It is very natural to go with the mainstream, to live the way other people live, to do what other people do, to believe what other people believe, and to speak what other people say. Anything that is popular and appeals to the five senses of man, we readily accept.

Sellers of goods and services take advantage of this behavior to make their businesses prosper. Satan also takes advantage of this behavior to entrap you as a victim of his corruptive schemes.

Corruption enters in your heart by tickling or stimulating your five senses to arouse the desire to feed the lust of your eyes, the lust of your flesh, and the pride of life. When corruption is established in you, it slowly spreads its influence through you to captivate others. Once it succeeds in establishing itself on a bigger scale, it becomes the norm, the trend, and everyone buys into it. It corrupts everything along its way. Corruption begets corruption. It establishes itself as the culture in that place among the people.

The apostle Peter reminded us to be sober and to watch carefully because our adversary, the devil, is patiently roaming around like a lion, always looking to capture victims to enslave them and destroy their lives. As Satan rebelled against God, so he is at every instance trying to catch his victim to serve his evil purposes. He desires to thwart the good plan God has for you and to prevent you from glorifying God in your life. He wants you to glorify him instead of God.

Corruption is at work in people's everyday lives: in their homes, in the streets, and in the marketplace. People are often bombarded with corrupting influences through television, movies, the Internet, and print media. Everyone is a targeted victim: young and old. Everywhere. Anytime.

Chapter 10

MY FRIEND

I REMEMBER A FRIEND who was so close to me and with whom I can identify myself as closely as if I am her shadow. Where she goes, I go; what she does, I do. There is no secret between the two of us. She knows everything about me, and I know her as thoroughly as I know myself. We both came from the same social background. We have similar upbringings and were raised in similar circumstances.

We became acquainted with each other in the workplace because we worked in the same office. Her job dealt with contracts administration, which involved everything concerning procurement: estimates, advertisement for tenders, prequalification of bidders, acceptance and opening of bids, evaluation of the bids received, and selection of the best bid for award. She had gained much experience in this line of work and had won the respect of her peers, immediate supervisors, and consultants. She always tried to do her work thoroughly, honestly, and without partiality. She did everything to give glory to God as if her boss was the Lord Jesus and not her human bosses (Col. 3:17).

Her life is a testimony of how true wisdom, loving fear of God, and hatred of all things that are evil and wrong helped her mitigate the corrupting influences surrounding her work. She resolved to herself not to be swept into the tide of the corrupting influences that are prevalent in the kind of work situation where she worked. She trusted in God's goodness and power, and she tried to maneuver herself through it with God's grace, doing her work and skirting the culture of corruption around her by not coming against the evil forces head-on but standing on the principles of the righteousness of God, doing what is right no matter what.

She knew the consequences of losing her job if she would not compromise with the workers of unrighteousness. But God proved to her the truth of His Word and His faithfulness time and time again, that as it is written, "The name of the Lord Jesus is a strong tower the righteous run into it and are safe" (Prov. 18:10). She did not fear, but trusted in the Lord her God to do His will. Therefore, she respected her superiors, but in the strength of the Lord she kept on doing good and thereby "put to silence the ignorance of foolish men" (1 Pet. 2:15) as best as she could.

And the Lord taught her how to knocked down the ugly heads of the corruptive influences that showed themselves to her in the course of her work. The Word of God proved what God said to her: "Who is the man that fears the Lord? Him shall He teach in the way He chooses" (Ps. 25:12). The Lord was faithful in His promises; He strengthened her, helped her, and upheld her with His "righteous right hand" (Isa. 40:10).

My friend's job was the envy of many who looked at it as a lucrative source of illegal income and of acquiring illegal wealth. Actually, she loved the work, as it challenged her to write clear and righteous contract bid documentations and specifications and allowed her to plug loopholes in the bid conditions and requirements relative to procurement and construction contracts by which the crafty may try to corrupt the procurement processes.

But she hated the culture of corruption which that kind of work usually attracts. She worked carefully and meticulously, always trying to please God and not man. She respected and honored her superiors, encouraged her subordinates, and was cordial toward the bidders so that they were not able to find anything against her to get her out of their way and out of her job. To her bosses, she was "obedient to, with fear and trembling, in sincerity of heart , as to Christ; not with eye service, as to please them, but as bondservant of Christ, doing the righteous will of God from the heart, with goodwill doing service, as to the Lord, and not to them" (Eph. 6:5–7, author's paraphrase). I saw from her life the truth of what God says in His Word, that "when a man's ways please the Lord, He makes even his enemies to be at peace with him" (Prov. 16:7).

My friend was already a widow when I came to know her. What she earned from her job was hardly enough to raise her children, so she had to make use of revolving loans from legal sources to bridge the financial gap for her children's needs. She also had to buy and sell small quantities of vegetables and fruits to augment her income.

She was made to discharge legally the functions of her job in an acting capacity for years, while the salary for discharging the duties for the actual position was withheld from her by her superiors. This is the manner the evil one works to squeeze you out of your resolve so you will join the band of the corrupted.

She wanted to leave her job to escape the corrupt environment and to earn a little more for her children's needs, and she tried to look for employment outside of that organization but was not successful. She almost got one job, but someone stood in the way for her not to be hired. When her husband died, the family income was reduced by two thirds. Her income at this time as a widowed mother was barely sufficient for her children's needs.

She was indeed situated in a perfectly vulnerable

situation to succumb to temptations from the corruptor. But she committed herself and her work to God and stayed on to do the job because she needed to earn a living. But God! He is good! The Lord upheld her through those years and provided what her children needed.

My friend found herself caught in situations similar to that we described in chapter one. She was aware of the corrupting influences around her and their work against her without letting up. Through it all, the hand of God delivered her from the corrupting influences and temptations she encountered. She continued to do her job in that environment for many years until God took her out of it and gave her a new assignment.

Here are some examples of the situations she encountered. I am writing them here for you as best as I can remember to show you there is something you can do to beat corruption.

One day a bidder who failed the prequalification requirements and was disqualified to bid for a project came to her office to try to resubmit his documents. As he handed her his papers, a crisp bill fell from the stack. My friend asked the man what the money was for. The man said nothing. She handed the money and the documents back to him. Then she noticed a gun, which was tucked and obviously bulging in his waistline, which the man's hand was rubbing, as if to call her attention to the gun. She calmly but firmly told the man she was not authorized to receive any payment and that the man should to go to the office cashier who was authorized to receive payments and could issue him a receipt for what he paid. Of course, the man knew he couldn't pay the cashier money that was meant for a bribe or grease and demand a receipt for it in return.

In another instance, she submitted a recommendation to her boss to award a bidder who offered compliance to the specifications and bid requirements, although his bid was the second-to-the-lowest bid. She discovered some officials did not agree with her recommendation and intended to give the award to the lowest bidder, despite his non-compliance to the conditions of tender.

On the day the committee deliberated about the award, her boss required her to sit down with them. She thought in her heart it was useless for her to be with them because they had already decided what they were going to do—that is, give the award to the lowest bidder despite his non-compliance. She respected her boss, but with heaviness in her heart went with him to the committee meeting. While the committee deliberated on the award for the defective bid, my friend sat quietly, meditating on the Word of God to Joshua: "Have I not commanded you? Be strong and of good courage; do not be dismayed, for the LORD your God is with you wherever you go" (Josh. 1:9).

When the members of the committee finally agreed to give the award to the lowest bidder, she felt the righteousness of God rise up in her and was stirred to talk. As words came out from her mouth, she said, "We ask for these requirements—1, 2, 3, etc.,—but this bidder offered otherwise—this, this, and this, etc." She enumerated the many requirements the bidder favored by the committee did not comply with.

There was complete silence after she spoke. My friend looked at everyone around the table. She composed and steadied herself to hear from them words of reprimand or rebuke. But no one said a word. She did not feel any fear. She felt the peace of God in her heart. The "perfect love" of God "cast out fear" from her heart (1 John 4:18).

The contract award went to the second-lowest-priced bid that complied with the requirements.

Satan attacks you when you are in your most vulnerable state and in your most difficult situation. It was during one of those times that he tried to tempt my friend with a big bribe. It was almost time for her kids to be enrolled in school. She had very little money left—not even enough to pay for her children's enrollment and food. After her husband's death, she made a claim for the proceeds of her husband's life insurance. However, she was not able to get the whole proceeds of his insurance because of a defect in the manner her husband designated his beneficiaries, which was not rectified while he was still alive. She needed money so badly for the children's schooling. During that time, in addition to selling fruits and vegetables, she tried to augment her income further by helping a friend sell specialty paints.

The temptation came to my friend in this manner. A person of authority in her organization called and offered her a "good" job. She thought he was giving her a good referral for the paint product she was selling. But it turned out that the job involved her conniving with a bidder whose bid was the third-lowest bid in a supply contract.

Through this intermediary, she was offered a down payment for a bribe for her participation in their scheme—if she said yes to the request. The amount offered as down payment would have been more than the proceeds of her husband's insurance that she was not able to collect as a lump-sum payment. According to this official, the "scrupulous bidder" promised to give her the balance of the bribe upon the award of the contract.

The offer was so tempting during that time of her need. The bribe would provide more than what she needed to send her children to school—and more—for a long time. What was asked of her was very easy to do. Aside from her work in contracts administration and the processing of bidders' qualifications and the evaluation of bids for award, she was also the custodian of all the records related to it.

This offer was a very subtle way of corrupting the bidding process. The bidder asked through the official, who had no direct responsibility for the procurement process, for my friend to give this bidder a copy of all the bids received through the official. This was all she needed to do. The bidder would do the evaluation of the bids on her behalf.

This indeed was an easy way to earn money unrighteously. But God had placed that fear of Him in my friend's heart. Her problem was only temporary. She thought to herself that if she allowed the corruptor to set her free from her "one-time problem," it will be the start of corruption's hold in her life. She would certainly continue to accept bribes and do corrupt things over and over again, "for by whom a person is overcome, by [it] also he is brought into bondage" (2 Pet. 2:19).

Furthermore, she thought if she fed her children the wages of corruption, they would also bear the fruit of corruption in their lives. She was afraid of the Word of the Lord, saying, "Every tree which does not bear good fruit is cut down and thrown into the fire" (Matt. 3:10). If she would do corrupt things, it would be as if she was "sowing the wind" and eventually would be "reaping the whirlwind" (Hos. 8:7) from her children's lives. She did not want her children to bear bad fruit and be corrupted as a consequence of allowing corruption in their lives.

As my friend drove home that night, she talked and cried her heart out to God. She asked Him a lot of "whys." Why was He giving this thing to her while she looked for another job outside the organization? Why God had not allowed her to collect the full benefits of her husband's insurance for her children's needs? Why she did not get that good-paying job she was considered for in another office when the manager who interviewed her asked her to report back to work after two weeks? Aside from her children's needs, her husband's death left her with a mortgage on their house for which, ironically, he failed to get mortgage insurance. She asked, Why? Why did her supervisors not appoint her as incumbent to that position she was performing in acting capacity? The salary for that position would have been enough for her need for the family's budget.

She was broken. And then the fear of God to do what is morally wrong and the fear of corruption's consequences in her children's lives dawned on her. It gave her understanding. She believed if she humbled herself under God's mighty hand He would raise her up in due time, for He cares for her and her children (1 Pet. 5:6–7; James 4:10). She thought that if she committed to do an evil thing, she would continue doing it and would be a servant to the Corruptor.

The Word of God spoke to her: "Do you not know that to whom you present yourselves to obey, you are that one's slave whom you obey, whether of sin leading to [corruption], or of obedience leading to righteousness?" (Rom. 6:16). In that moment, she submitted herself, her children, and their situation into God's hands. She decided to trust in God.

The next day, she called that official and told him,

"Thank you for your concern about me. I am afraid to do what you asked me to do. I am sorry, but I cannot do it."

The Bible says, "When a man's ways please the LORD, he makes even his enemies to be at peace with him" (Prov. 16:7). The official who tried to entice her to the bribe kept silent. He and whoever was in agreement with him knew that my friend's moral principle was founded on the righteousness that comes from God.

But I saw God do more than this concerning my friend. Two days later, the bidder who made the offer of the bribe to my friend through the official personally visited my friend in her office. He apologized to her, saying he was very, very sorry. My friend told him, "You really ought to be sorry. If you submitted a good bid, you could win the contract. I have not done anything before like what you asked, and I am not doing it now, nor will I do it in the future."

The bidder bowed before her with his head almost touching the floor to show his sincerity and respect to my friend. People from the country where this man came from have the custom of bowing to show their respect to someone highly regarded. But it was the first time I had observed it.

I knew it was not to my friend that he was really bowing to. He bowed to the presence of the righteous God he saw in the testimony of my friend. The Bible says, "The evil will bow before the good, and the wicked at the gates of the righteous" (Prov. 14:19). Every knee shall bow to God, even the devil that works Corruption in the hearts of man, and in the world. "At the name of Jesus every knee should bow, of those in heaven, and of those on earth, and of those under the earth, and that every tongue should confess that Jesus Christ is Lord, to the glory of God the Father" (Phil. 2:10–11).

How I wish there were more people like my friend who have the fear of God in their hearts, who can be entrusted with the kind of job that attracts corruptors as moths are attracted to the light! If there were more like her, corruption could be overcome if not totally eradicated.

You may ask me then, "How was your friend able to support and send her children to school?" Remember that my friend was selling specialty paints to augment her income? Up to the time she was offered that big bribe, she had not sold any paint products yet. She tried to offer the paint to others who weren't clients or bidders dealing with her office, and she avoided doing things that would result in a conflict of interest in connection with her job. She trusted in God and His words, for He said to her, "I will preserve the lives of your children, they are father-less; and you, trust in Me for you are a widow" (Jer. 49:11, author's paraphrase). So, she "trusted in the Lord with all her heart, and leaned not on her own understanding; In all her ways she acknowledged Him, and He directed her paths" (Prov. 3:5-6, author's paraphrase).

And the "Lord did awesome things for her for which she did not look" (Isa. 64:3, author's paraphrase). God said, "My thoughts are not your thoughts nor are My ways your ways. For as the heavens are higher than the earth so are My ways higher than your ways and My thoughts than your thoughts" (Isa. 55:8).

A few days afterward, a friend and former officemate visited my friend in her office. She asked him if they had projects that needed anti-corrosion paints. He said, "No, but we needed roofing sheets that can withstand corrosion." He told her they were building structures near the seashore.

Like a flash of lightning, God placed this thought in her mind: "Why not paint anti-corrosion paint on the roofing sheets?"

She asked for the name of the builder, who turned out to be one of her former classmates in engineering school. Then she made two phone calls. First, she called her former classmate and asked if she could refer to him someone who could supply his requirement for anti-corrosion roofing. Next, she called the friend who is the supplier of the anti-corrosion paint to tell him about the prospect of supplying roofing sheets painted with anti-corrosion paint for her classmate's project. The paint supplier then called her classmate and made arrangements with him for supplying the anti-corrosion roofing sheets. He also made arrangement with the millers for the roofing sheets to be painted with the paint he sold.

God placed a thought in my friend's mind to prosper her. He appointed her classmate to cross her life at this exact time. He provided the former officemate to connect her with her classmate. He provided the anti-corrosion paints from her friend who sold them, and the millers too! It was like a big puzzle that God perfectly provided for the pieces to fit together so amazingly and perfectly and at just the right time to help my friend out of her problem.

Glory to God! God made possible a big supply contract, and He provided for my friend and her children's needs. She did not even see what those roofing sheets looked like, but God saw everything from afar off and made everything possible. He appointed all the circumstances and provided a way for my friend to be delivered from the evils of corruption. In doing so, He also provided for her and her children's needs in a righteous way. God made all things worked out together for the good of my friend and her children because of her loving fear of God into which she was called as He had purposed for her (Rom. 8:28).

Truly, the word of God says, "He who did not spare His own Son, but delivered Him up for us all, how shall He not with Him also freely give us all things?" (Rom. 8:32). God provided help to my friend in an amazing way because she set her heart not to compromise with the workers of corruption but to trust in Him. God can do the same awesome thing for you if you will obey and trust Him.

The Bible says, "The LORD will teach a man who fears Him and teach him in the way He chooses" (Ps. 25:12). My friend humbled herself under the mighty hand of God, trusted in Him, and submitted herself and her children's case to Him. And the Father knew the things my friend had need of and had already provided for it even before she asked Him. (Matt. 6:8), for "the Lord is good, a stronghold in the day of trouble; And He knows those who trust in Him" (Nah. 1:7).

After the temptation by the mediator failed to draw my friend into corruption, it became evident to everyone that my friend was working within that office her "pattern of good works; in doctrine showing integrity, reverence, incorruptibility, sound speech that cannot be condemned, that one who is an opponent may be ashamed, having nothing evil to say" of her (Tit. 2:7–8).

But the workers of unrighteousness "do not sleep unless they have done evil; and their sleep is taken away unless they make someone fall" (Prov. 4:16) and "sets himself in a way that is not good. He does not abhor evil" (Ps. 36:4). As my friend had said before, those workers of corruption do not stop their work and will find ways to pursue their evil purpose in trapping men by tempting them to join them in their corruptive ways.

Those who were behind the attempt to bribe my friend

looked for someone else to do it for them. Another person was assigned to evaluate that particular bid. My friend was relieved of responsibility in the evaluation of this particular project. All documents related to that tender were taken from her.

But when the recommendation for award came out, she was not surprised to find that the award was made to the bidder who had said sorry to her. It did surprise her to see the award price to be more than 30 percent higher than the bidder's original bid and for the bid to include additional items that were not part of the requested tender.

Her name was included in the listed names of people recommending the award, and the award was passed to her for signature, but she abstained from signing it. She returned the award document without her signature, and her immediate boss and the committee chairman called and asked her to sign it. She declined and told them her reason for not signing, and the award for that supply contract was finalized and approved without her signature.

Could it be that it was not a bidder who financed the expenses to corrupt the bidding process but actually the office who called for the bidding? Could it be that corrupted people get their wages of corruption from the office but indirectly from the hand of the bidder? These people did not dip their hands directly into the coffers of the office, but they were aiding the bidder to defraud the office and gain illegal profit by doing so. Could this be the reason that poverty exists around the world? People ultimately and eventually are paying for and will have to pay for the price of corruption. The generations after you and even those after them that are yet to come will bear the impact of corruption that is happening right now.

This is the way of corruption. It is just like the way of the octopus as it hunts for its prey. The very life of the octopus is hunting for its prey to gobble it up as it continues to grow bigger; so it is with the workers of corruption: their very nature is to corrupt and to implement their corruptive schemes to satisfy their lusts. They will always find a way to do it. They will always find someone to agree to do it for them and with them.

With her superiors knowing her stand against corruption and yet seeing no way to fault her and to remove her from her work and with no job offers from other employers, my friend had no choice but to stay and continue working in that office. But the superiors in her office who knew her stand against corruption did everything they could to make sure she held her job in an acting capacity, so she was not paid commensurately for the job she was doing.

All through those years, she tried to find another job outside that organization, but she was not successful. How she managed to stay on doing that job, it is only by the grace of God who had placed her there to do that job for a season and a reason. She humbled herself and trusted in God. Again, He taught her how to "trust in Him with all her heart, and not to lean on her own understanding; in all her ways for her to acknowledge Him; and so He directed her paths" (Prov. 3:5–6, author's paraphrase).

At the end of that long time in the wilderness, the Lord told my friend to leave that job, saying, "Depart! Depart! Go out from there. Touch no unclean thing; go out from the midst of her, be clean, you who bear the vessels of the Lord. For you shall not go out with haste, nor go by flight; for the Lord will go before you, and He will be your rear guard" (Isa. 52:11–12). My friend struggled at the thought of leaving that job with no prospect of another job and no source of income to support her children's needs, but she knew that she should heed the voice of the Lord, and she submitted to Him. She submitted her papers to quit the job. She trusted in the Lord. And the Lord gave her peace.

And yet the Lord surprised her by His amazing ways again! God proved Himself to her that His way is perfect; He proved to her His word is true. He proved that He is a shield to her because she trusted in Him (2 Sam. 22:31).

The day after she had submitted her papers to leave the job, she received a call from another employer offering her to work with them beginning the following week. And this time, in that new job, the Lord revealed to my friend why He kept her in her old job for what appeared to her to be a very long journey in the desert. In her old job, the Lord taught her humility even to her superiors from whom she did not find favor because of her moral convictions to fear to do anything wrong. The Lord showed her how the world works and how corruption will always try to encroach in the workplace. She learned to trust in God and His Word. Her supervisors looked down upon her so much so that she was often bypassed in such a way that projects that should normally passed through her were directly assigned to her subordinates, and then from her subordinates back to the superiors. Those were very hurting times for her, but they were occasions that strengthened her faith in God and in His Word.

In this new job assignment, the Lord shifted my friend from working from a "tail situation" into working from a "head situation." She was assigned to work with a group that was evaluating the operation of organizations that this group was supporting or helping, and her previous office was one of them.

My friend became aware that some people from her previous office tried to remove her from her new employment because she knew so many things about their office. Maybe it was their way to continue to persecute her for not being identified with them or maybe it was because of her understanding of how corruption can entrench itself in an organization's conduct of its business. She had no idea. But their efforts did not prosper. The Word of God says, "The name of the LORD is a strong tower; the righteous run to it and are safe" (Prov. 18:10). She proved this over and over during those long years of working in that corruptive environment. The Lord was her "rock" and her "fortress. He "led and guided" her and "pulled" her out of the net which they had secretly laid for her, for He was her "strength" (Ps. 31:3–4).

With this new employment, the Lord restored almost three hundred times to my friend what she had lost during the long years working with her previous employer. The Lord gave her more than what she needed for her family. The Lord filled her with joy, with fatness, and with peace because she had hungered for God's righteousness for which she was previously persecuted by those whom she served. (See Matthew 5:6, 10, author's paraphrase.)

Chapter 11

THE EFFECTS
OF CORRUPTION

FTER MY FRIEND rejected the offer of bribery, she refused to involve herself in the evaluation process of that particular call for tender. She knew how desperate the parties of corruption can be. They will do everything to have their way.

It was no surprise for her to see that particular bidder awarded the contract for that tender. But she was surprised when she found out that the cost of the contract awarded to the bidder was more than 30 percent higher than what the bidder had originally offered in his bid.

A question that bothered her was, "Could the difference between the higher contract cost and the bidder's original bid price be the representation expense—the bribes paid to whoever was involved in making the award of contract possible?" If there were people who received bribes, they did not get money directly from the coffers of the organization, but they might indirectly have received the bribe from the bidder. The bidder might not have actually lost anything from the illegal transaction. Whatever amount he might have paid as a bribe might have been added to the cost of his contract. The loser in the corrupted transaction is the organization or the office who called for the tender.

Organizations in the public sector or in the private sector operate on a budget in the conduct of their operations. When the actual expenditures exceed that which has been set aside or budgeted for any contract or activity, the tendency is to look for ways to cover up the deficit. The ways governments cover the deficit is by increasing taxes, cutting the cost from other budgeted expense accounts, reducing the quality and extent of the services it provides, or by eliminating some of the services it provides in order to offset the deficit. In the private sector, the cost of corruption impacts the quality and the cost of goods and services provided to clients and consumers, resulting in higher cost and/or diminished quality of goods.

The final effects of corruption are eventually passed on to the people: customers, clients, and users. The people are impacted by the increase in the cost of goods and services, the reduction in the quality of goods, the extent and quality of services, and the higher taxes. Consumers, clients, and users have to spend more to procure their needs because of the imputed cost of corruption. Whether you like it or not, you will experience that the gap between the cost of living and your purchasing power is getting bigger and bigger. Generally, the number of people getting poorer and poorer is increasing. Additionally, the extent and degree of poverty around the world continues to slide down. Jesus said, "You have the poor with you always" (Mark 14:7). Jesus foretold this because He knew that Satan, who is the power behind corruption, will never stop keeping people in bondage to sin and poverty.

Corruption is like a continuing whirlwind. It sucks everything around it. It seems to be an incurable and hopeless situation. It pulls back economic activity. It keeps on adding to and impacting the cost of living in societies and stretches the moral fiber of society as it causes the degeneration of established moral principles. It causes people to lose trust and respect in their government and in established laws. It makes governance ineffective. It causes the breakup of families. It causes demoralization in organizations and in societies. It seeps into and incorporates itself in the culture of a society. It makes government ineffective and breeds further demoralization and corruption. Corruption has an idol enshrined in it: *greed!*

As an example, consider the story of the first man to walk the length of the Amazon River—6,700 kilometers—which he completed in 860 days. His name is Ed Stafford, and he is a British citizen. Stafford says the journey "has deepened his understanding of the Amazon, its role in protecting the globe against climate change and the complex forces that are leading to its destruction.... He has seen vast swaths of demolished jungle.... 'It's the people in power who are benefitting from the extraction of the natural resources here.... That's why there are corrupt politicians and laws that aren't enforced and loads of unconstrained deforestation still going on.'"[1]

As we read the news of floods and landslides occurring in many places, we wonder if these natural calamities could be the effect of irresponsible denudation of forests that were triggered by activities linked to corruption? The people—especially the poor—bear the brunt of the after-effects of this corruption.

The main objective of Satan is to totally corrupt man—his heart, his thoughts, and his ways of living—and to push him deeper into the pit of destruction and poverty and away from God. Those who do wickedly against the covenant, he shall corrupt with flattery; but the people who know their God shall be strong, and carry out great exploits (Dan. 11:32).

The effects and cost of corruption as it impacts the people—the consumers and the users of the goods and services and the government—cannot be quantified. The end users are the people in societies and people groups.

The impact of corruption occurring in the public and the private sector organizations and in the marketplaces are passed on directly to people in societies in the form of increased cost and/or reduction in the quality of goods, reduced purchasing power, skewed economies, general apathy to government rule, lowered moral standards and goals, and lawlessness. When data is suppressed, as we learned in chapter five, the amount of tax defrauded from the government impacts the government's funding capacity and ability to operate well and provide the necessary services to the people.

The additional expense incurred to finance corruption in any manner is absorbed by the consumers and users of goods and services: the people. When governments are affected, the consequential effects of corruption are passed on to the people one way or another through lower quality services or higher taxes. Corruption and its evil effects cause much suffering, poverty, hunger, injustice, lawlessness, and hopelessness to many around the world. The net impact of corruption is poverty in the world!

You might wonder, "Could corruption be what triggered the start of the financial crisis of 2008 and the ensuing economic meltdown of many countries in the world?" We continue to live in uncertain times caused by the "shaking up" of the economies of the world. Businesses are closing. People are losing jobs. Living conditions have gone down, and are still going down. Many of the poor are getting mired in deeper and deeper poverty. Social problems are getting more and more difficult to address. People are getting hopeless.

God saved Noah and his family from the flood that destroyed the corrupted people of his time. When he came out of the ark, Noah built an altar to the Lord and offered a sacrifice. The Lord was pleased and promised to "never again curse the ground for man's sake," although man's heart is evil, "nor destroy every living thing as He had done." God also promised, "While the earth remains, seedtime and harvest, cold and heat, and day and night shall not cease" (Gen. 8:15–22). God is faithful to His promises, but He needs a response from you before He does His part.

You cannot be like Jonah who tried to avoid God's instruction to warn the people of Nineveh of impending doom if they will not return to the living God (see Jon. 1). God pities those who live their lives carelessly, not discerning between good or evil. He is "not willing that any should perish but that all should come to repentance" (2 Pet. 3:9). Let us tell people the way out of corruption and poverty is through the saving grace of Jesus Christ.

Chapter 12

DOES GOD ALLOW CORRUPTION?

Y OU MAY ASK, "If God is a good God and if He is holy, why does He allow corruption, which is bad and evil, to happen?" Of course, you are thinking that a good God can never allow something bad to happen. I have also struggled to find an answer to this question—until I opened my Bible and God gave me understanding from His Word.

The Bible, the written Word of God, gives the answer to these questions. "The Lord is good, a stronghold in the day of trouble; and He knows those who trust in Him" (Nah. 1:7). Also, "The Lord is longsuffering toward us, not willing that any should perish but that all should come to repentance" (2 Pet. 3:9). One definition of the word "perish" in *Merriam-Webster's Dictionary* is "to become destroyed or ruined." From this definition, we infer that God is not willing that anyone be destroyed or ruined by corruption. In chapter three of this book, we learned that corruption is being in the state of rottenness or in the process of rotting. Of course, God does not want you or anyone else to be corrupted, to be ruined, or to be rotten. You are His special creation. As He created Adam after His own image, so were you also created in His own image.

It is not our parents who created us: "It is He who made us" (Ps. 100:3). God used our parents so we could be brought forth into the world. The Bible says, "He formed your inward parts; He covered you in your mother's womb. You are fearfully and wonderfully made in His marvelous way. Your frame was not hidden from Him, when He made you in secret; and He skillfully fashioned you when you are not yet here on earth. His eyes saw you even when you are not yet formed. And even then He had already determined your days even when you are not yet" (Ps. 139:13–16, author's paraphrase).

You may ask again, "If I am fearfully and wonderfully made by God in His marvelous way, then why does He allow corruption in the world which can ruin me, His special creation?"

God's desire for you is holiness. It is written, "Be holy, for I am holy" (1 Pet. 1:16). God did not allow corruption so you could be corrupted. Corruption was present in the universe because of Satan's sin of pride and rebellion against God even before Adam existed. Satan was the first one who sinned and corrupted himself. As a result of his sin, God banished him out of His presence and cast him out of heaven. Satan continues to impose his usurped dominion authority on the earth and rule as the god of the air and this world system. He works tirelessly to capture as many of us as possible to be partakers of his corrupt and evil ways.

God does not want you to be corrupted and to be rotten and eventually to perish. God says, "Understand and know Me. I am the Lord, exercising lovingkindness, judgment, and righteousness in the earth, for in these I delight" (Jer. 9:24, author's paraphrase). God wants you to be with Him where he is, in heaven, for all eternity. For even in the beginning, he had planned for Adam to live in the garden with a life that is sin-free, carefree, prosperous, peaceful, and joyful. God says, "You shall be holy, for I the Lord your God am holy" (Lev. 19:2). But by your own efforts, it is difficult to be holy and to be with God in heaven because, again, "All have sinned and fall short of the glory of God" (Rom. 3:23).

But God has given us a hope: "To [you] God willed to make known what are the riches of the glory of the mystery [which has been hidden among those who do not know Him]: which is Christ in you, the hope of glory" (Col. 1:27).

He has given us a Deliverer: And the Lord will deliver [you] from every evil work [of corruption] and preserve [you] for His heavenly kingdom" (2 Tim. 4:18).

He has given us a Savior: Christ, the Savior of the world. When the angel of the Lord announced the birth of Jesus to the shepherds who were out in the field, the angel said, "Do not be afraid, for behold, I bring you good tidings of great joy which will be to all people. For there is born to you this day in the city of David a Savior, who is Christ the Lord" (Luke 2:8–11).

God has given us a Redeemer who can save us from corruption in the Person of Jesus. He lived on this earth in human flesh yet was without sin because He is perfect God and perfect Man. He has redeemed you with His blood and bought you back from the hand of Satan. He gave you His life. He died in your place. He shed His blood for you so you can have victory over the corruptive schemes of the devil. He did it completely, once and for all, for everyone.

It is not only difficult but totally impossible for you, in your own strength, to be holy as God commands. My friend whose testimony against corruption was given in chapter ten had discovered that it was only by the grace of God that she could be delivered from giving in to the tempting offer of that big bribe. She discovered the secret source of strength that helped her overcome corruption: Christ in her, the hope of glory! (Col. 1:27). She submitted herself and her cares to Jesus because she knew that He cares for her and her children (1 Pet. 5:7). And she heeded the apostle Peter's warning that said, "Be sober, be vigilant; because your adversary the devil walks about like a roaring lion, seeking whom he may devour. Resist him, steadfast in the faith, knowing that the same sufferings are experienced by [others] in the world" (1 Pet. 5:8–9). Thus, she resisted the temptations of corruption in her life.

The situation my friend encountered is happening in too many places in the world. Perhaps you are also facing some of those situations which she had encountered. Or perhaps you resisted Satan's scheme with your own strength and were overcome by his tricks. You might think that now it is too late to go back to where you were before. Listen! There is no such thing as too late or a lost chance with God! God never runs out of grace; His mercy never ends. He loves you so much that He gave His only begotten Son, so that if you will believe in Him you shall be saved from corruption and receive everlasting life. (John 3:16, paraphrased)

At Calvary, Jesus was crucified between two criminals who hanged on their own crosses. However these two criminals were there because of their own evil deeds. One of them blasphemed Jesus, while the other one rebuked the other criminal. In his last hour, this thief repented of his wrong deeds and asked Jesus, saying, "'Lord remember me when You come into Your kingdom.' And Jesus said to him, 'Assuredly, I say to you, today you will be with Me in Paradise'" (Luke 23:42–43). God's grace and mercy are available to anyone, at any time, even in the last hour of their life. God is faithful. He hears and answers your prayers. He will hear you and answer you now if you come to Him in humility and pray this prayer:

> *Lord Jesus, thank You that You are rich in grace and mercy. I acknowledge before You my sins. I blindly followed the ways of the ruler of this world that led my life's direction opposite of Your way of righteousness. Lord, forgive me for following the corrupted ways of the evil one. Let Your love, Lord, cover the deeds I have done against Your will. Lead me to live in Your way of truth and life. Christ, live in me and be my hope of glory. Thank You, Jesus. Amen.*

Chapter 13

MITIGATING CORRUPTION

CORRUPTION IS LIKE a tree. It will not die unless its roots are completely destroyed; otherwise, new growth of its kind will regrow again and again from its stump.

In order to fight and eradicate corruption, we need to know its root and the manner in which it operates. In the previous chapters, you have read why and how corruption happens and who is behind it. The people who fall prey to corruption—the corrupted and the corruptor—are not your enemies. They are people blinded and deceived by the devil to obey his will. Remember, "you do not [fight] against flesh and blood, but against principalities, against powers, against the rulers of the darkness of this age, against spiritual hosts of wickedness in the heavenly places" (Eph. 6:12).

The real enemy and power behind corruption is Satan who is the god of this world system. He induces corruption and fuels its growth in the world by his principles of unrighteous control with the use of might, greed, pride, lust, and deception. Satan is "like a roaring lion seeking whom to devour" (1 Pet. 5:8), not only those who are easy prey for him but also those who oppose him.

Fighting corruption head-on in your own ability is difficult. It is only in the name of Jesus and the power of His blood and the might of His Holy Spirit that we can defeat Satan and overcome his works of corruption. You can overcome corruption only if you resist Satan in the strength and power God will give you if you submit to Him. You "can do all things through Christ who [empowers] you" (Phil. 4:13), and Jesus said, "Without Me you can do nothing" (John 15:5).

Corruption is a social disease that has grown so big and formidable, it is like an octopus with long tentacles waving in every direction seeking its prey. Corruption enslaves people who are willing to be corrupted by the Corruptor, and it pushes the poor deeper and deeper into poverty. Even innocent people the world over are affected by corruption. There is so much poverty and suffering in the world today, as studies in corruption have revealed.

Corruption's evil powers loom over the management

of government and private businesses. It operates in the corridors of power in organizations, establishing its hold in the hearts of selfish men who are greedy for gain at the expense of others. Corruption threatens and impacts societies in the world with its corrupting influences that lead to poverty, moral degradation, social problems, and lawlessness.

Many leading organizations and groups had awakened to the urgency of the need to mitigate corruption in order to lessen its disastrous impact to the world. These organizations observe, gather information, and analyze the problems caused by corruption, especially in countries where corruption has established visible strongholds. These organizations come up with good recommendations on how to curtail the growth of corruption, and they suggest solutions to prevent and to mitigate its occurrence and to curtail its growth.

Some of the more visible of these organizations have succeeded in starting to mitigate corruption in the world are as follows.

The United Nations (UN)

The United Nations initiated the UN Convention against Corruption (UNCAC) in 2003, which is a global treaty among state signatories and the first legally binding anticorruption framework in the world. It required signatories to sign a convention to set broad and clear anti-corruption measures in the laws of their home countries. As of March 1, 2011, 140 signatories and 150 parties to the convention had ratified, accepted, approved, acceded, or succeeded to the framework.[1]

The highlights of the UNCAC convention include prevention, criminalization, international cooperation, and asset recovery related to corruption around the world. One of its benefits includes a mechanism for the need to protect witnesses, reporting persons and victims of corruption.[2] It also recognizes the role of the private sector and of private sector corruption as part of the problem.

ORGANISATION FOR ECONOMIC CO-OPERATION AND DEVELOPMENT (OECD)

The Organisation for Economic Co-operation and Development began in 1961 with the purpose of stimulating economic progress and world trade in the aftermath of World War II. In the words of the OECD, "The common thread of our work is a shared commitment to market economies backed by democratic institutions and focused on the wellbeing of all citizens. Along the way, we also set out to make life harder for the terrorists, tax dodgers, crooked businessmen and others whose actions undermine a fair and open society."[3]

The OECD has helped coordinate international action against corruption and bribery through its creation of the OECD Anti-Bribery Convention, which came into effect in February 1999. This convention "establishes legally binding standards to criminalise bribery of foreign officials in international business transactions and provides for a host of related measures that make this effective."[4] However, its role is limited to monitoring and not implementation.

MILLENNIUM CHALLENGE CORPORATION (MCC)

The Millennium Challenge Corporation is a United States agency established in January 2004 aimed at reducing global poverty. It "forms partnerships with some of the world's poorest countries, but only those committed to good governance, economic freedom, and investment in their citizens."[5] One of the key programs of the MCC is the fight against corruption in the work toward global poverty reduction. Specifically, "MCC uses the World Bank Institute's Control of Corruption indicator as part of its selection criteria…this indicator measures the frequency of 'additional payments to get things done,' the effects of corruption on the business environment, 'grand corruption' in the political arena, and the tendency of elites to engage in 'state capture.'"[6]

The World Bank

The World Bank, based in Washington, DC, provides loans, credits, and grants to developing countries in an effort to "fight poverty with passion and professionalism for lasting results."[7] Additionally, "the Bank has identified corruption as among the greatest obstacles to economic and social development."[8] Since 1996, the Bank has supported more than 600 anti-corruption initiatives around the world.

Global Organization of Parliamentarians Against Corruption (GOPAC)

GOPAC is a not-for-profit organization founded in 2002 that brings parliamentarians around the world together for the sole purpose of fighting corruption. Founded by John Williams, retired Member of Parliament from Canada, GOPAC seeks to move beyond mere dialogue to deliver results.[9]

Transparency International (TI)

Transparency International is an advocacy global network with more than ninety national chapters in countries around the world. The organization is a leader in the momentum for global advocacy against corruption. It seeks the involvement and participation of governments, the private sector, civil organizations, and the media for the purpose of improving the conduct of business mostly in the government sector.[10]

World Economic Forum (WEF)

The World Economic Forum is "an independent international organization committed to improving the state of the world by engaging...leaders in partnerships to shape global, regional and industry agendas."[11] The WEF was established in 1971 and is non-political, non-partisan, impartial, and not for profit. It is comprised of world business leaders who hold no ties to any government.

The most significant achievement of the WEF in the fight against corruption is its Partnering Against Corruption Initiative (PACI). PACI brings the convening power of the World Economic Forum to bear on global businesses, gaining access to businesses that would otherwise be too difficult to reach, and offers them an opportunity to be counted among those taking a stand against corruption.

MORE AND MORE VOICES

As you can see from the list above—which is by no means exhaustive—people are rising up from almost everywhere and answering the call to fight corruption. They are adding their voices and contributing creative ideas in order to mitigate corruption.

One of these voices is Mr. Cielito Habito, a former cabinet minister in the Philippine government during the administration of President Ramos, who writes a column for a daily newspaper in Manila. His article, "No Free Lunch," published on June 29, 2010, the day before the inauguration of the new Philippine president in a time of unrest and loss of faith in government in the Philippines, is worthy of consideration. The suggestions offered by Mr. Habito here are practical and can be used in conjunction with guidelines proposed by other anti-corruption groups.

When it comes to restoring faith in government, Mr. Habito suggests that the people would hope to see:

- Quality appointments to key government posts of competent individuals of unquestionable reputation without regard for political affiliation.

- A clear-cut policy against corruption and leaders committed to lead by example to enforce it.

- Convincing practice of transparency and accountability, starting with enactment of a Freedom of Information Act.

- Simplification of centralized governance and development processes and greater involvement of local government units.

- Wider and deeper public participation in governance and development processes.

- Streamlined frontline government processes and procedures to eliminate cost-inducing and superfluous requirements.[12]

The possibility of committing corruption may be further reduced by appointing capable individuals of proven integrity to key and sensitive positions, such as those dealing with procurement, licensing, certifications, loan applications, standards and qualifications, the police, and the military. Training and development ought to be provided not only for organizational functions but for moral consciousness and responsibility. Corrupt practices can also be discouraged through the improvement of working conditions and benefits, performance reviews, and rotation of key level and line assignments. Clearly written guidelines, criteria, and objectives to implement the above will be helpful and can be offered with civil participation.

Top leadership should govern with wisdom and lead by example so as not to jeopardize their stance against corruption. They should not be leading blindly but should be aware of everything happening in the organization so as not to derail their efforts in mitigating corruption. Regular performance reports and audits against predetermined deliverables and doable results are useful not only in gauging accomplishments but also in checking for corruptive weaknesses in the organization. The auditing responsibility should be conducted by auditors who aren't beholden to the leadership of the government institutions they audit.

Promotion comes from God; He lifts one up (Dan. 2:21). As most leaders in government are elected by the people, so they are accountable to God by serving the people who elected them with honesty and moral discipline. Government leadership should be characterized by servanthood and service should not be motivated by selfish gain.

Most countries may not have legislation providing freedom to access information. In its absence, it is very easy to hide the conduct of public sector businesses. Its absence may contribute to hiding of corrupt practices that are occurring.

Decentralization, devolution of government processes,

and the streamlining of the processes it involved will eliminate redundant requirements or loopholes the corruptor and the corrupted take advantage of, thus eliminating the tendency to corrupt.

The aspect of mitigating corruption in the private sector will be more complicated, as there are many players involved and competition to profit plays a very important factor in their operation. This needs a more comprehensive study and research with the involvement of the wider business sector, the government, and the people.

The fight against corruption is difficult but important. It is physical and spiritual. Fighting corruption in your own strength and ability is dangerous. The battle is for the hearts of men. The battlefield is the world. The weapons used by Satan in this battle are deception, greed, lust, and pride. There are people you may think are the corrupted ones, but in reality they are pawns, robots powered by the evil power of the Corruptor, Satan. They have fallen into the deceptions of the evil one and were captured by him in their sins. Remember, you "are not fighting against flesh and blood [people] but against principalities, against powers, against the rulers of the darkness of this age, against spiritual hosts of wickedness in the heavenly places" (Eph. 6:12).

There are always two parties to corruption: the corruptor and the corrupted. Corruption will not prosper without one or the other. While we would like to see corruption eliminated in the public sector and the private sector, it is wishful thinking to think that the tribe of corruptors will grow less and less, for there will be no corruptors if there is no one to corrupt, and vice versa.

In order to mitigate corruption, you need to use a different kind of strategy: "For though [you] walk in the flesh, [you] do not war according to the flesh. For the weapons of [your] warfare are not carnal but mighty in God for pulling down strongholds, casting down arguments and every high thing that exalts itself against the knowledge of God, bringing every thought into captivity to the obedience of Christ, and being ready to punish all disobedience when your obedience is fulfilled" (2 Cor. 10:3–6).

Chapter 14

CAN CORRUPTION BE DEFEATED?

FROM THE PREVIOUS chapters of this book, we saw what corruption really is and how it affects governments, private enterprises, international trade, people, and societies. We also learned the works of Satan to establish corruption to control the world. We learned that Satan is the real power behind corruption as the god of this present world system. Satan is our real enemy. He is behind those corrupted people you may think are your enemies.

These chapters discussed the weapons and strategies the devil uses to induce corruption. He corrupts by arousing the lust of the flesh, the lust of the eyes, and the boosting of your pride. He will lift your self-esteem by offering baits to lure you. These things are good and necessary but are used in the wrong way to tempt you into corruption. Most people fall into the trap of the corruptor and are destroyed because of their lack of knowledge between right and wrong (Hos. 4:6) and the absence of the fear of God in their hearts.

Once established, corruption grows so fast. It satiates the corrupted of its wages, and it destoys because the devil behind it is "like a roaring lion, seeking whom he may devour" (1 Pet. 5:8). Corruption is never satisfied. It continues its rampage far beyond the places and lives upon which it had established its hold. It tries to control everything in its way.

Corruption is addictive. If left unchecked, it becomes like a cancer growing beyond control, affecting even the blameless. It affects everything good. It is decadent. Eventually, it seeps like water through a small opening in a dike, seeking its way forward until it breaks the norms of conduct and people's respect for each other's God-given rights. It becomes a way of life for everyone, and eventually it is accepted as normal. The moment you fall into its trap, you will crave more and more of its fruit to indulge the lust of the eyes, the lust of the flesh, and the greed for pride and power.

Corruption had grown to such a degree that in some cases it had become a malady that attacks not only the government, the private sector organizations, the economy of countries, and the lives of people in societies, but also the coming generations. It affects not only the country where it operates but also other countries that conduct trade with that country. In this age, no country is an island. The world is one big island.

The seed of corruption is easily planted and grows in the hearts of men. It breeds fast in man's sinful nature. Men who aren't content seek for more and more of the wealth, material things, and prestige of this world.

Again, there are two parties in the corruption cycle: the corruptor and the corrupted. Theirs is a mutual co-existence. One desires selfish advantage and the other one lusts for selfish gain. This is how Satan, the Corruptor and god of this world system, entraps you in his corrup-tive ways: either as the corruptor, or as the corrupted. "The heart is deceitful above all things, and desperately wicked"—only God knows it (Jer. 17:9). "Truly the hearts of the sons of men are full of evil; madness is in their hearts while they live" (Eccl. 9:3).

A man who fears God will hate to do evil. Satan will have a hard time tempting such a man to fall into his trap.

In chapter two of this book, I recalled the dwarf-like creatures I saw in the field from the window while I sat on my father's lap. They were walking back and forth in the moonlight. I felt no fear when I saw those dwarves because I was safely seated on my father's lap. Could God have opened my eyes then and let me see the reality that Satan had helpers, his demons or bad angels? And it amazed me how God had allowed me to remember that vision even after so many years.

Yes, the Bible tells us there is a hosts of fallen angels who took sides with Lucifer when he revolted against God. They are demons who help Satan. They work in the hearts of men to tempt them with baits for the lust of the flesh, the lust of the eyes, and the pride of life. Unless God is in control of your life, your desire is easily conceived through demonic thoughts used to trigger these lusts. Then, when your desire is activated, corruption gets a foothold in your life.

Chapter ten of this book tells the story of how my friend overcame the corrupting influences in her work situation. I shared just three of her many encounters with the agents of corruption she experienced in her many years of work. She determined in her heart to stand on her conviction to do what was morally right because of her loving fear of and obedience to the God who hates everything evil. She stood against corruption, and God safely delivered her out of its rottenness because she loved Him and hated the evil that God hates. She also trusted in His goodness.

Perhaps the story of my friend encouraged you as it encouraged me. Perhaps it helped you see hope in your fight against corruption.

Yet you will still see corruption's ugly head rearing itself from time to time in the conduct of business in many countries around the world. In spite of the positive response of anti-corruption organizations and some governments to tackle head-on the evils of corruption, it continues to proliferate. Corruption's corroding impact further pushes the world's population into deepening poverty and hopelessness and the world into a more troubled and chaotic situation.

You may ask, "Can corruption really be defeated?" The answer to your question is yes! Yes, we can defeat corruption if we do not give up the fight to claim the victory that Jesus Christ won on the cross over Satan, the Corruptor, the originator and author of corruption.

On the Cross, the sins of mankind were nailed with Jesus on His hands and His feet. Your wicked works and your wicked walks were nailed with Jesus on the Cross. Jesus provided a way for you to escape the corrupting influences of Satan and defeat corruption. Jesus bore your sins on His body on the Cross. He died on your behalf so that you may escape the death that you deserved because of your sins: "He Himself is the propitiation for [your sins], and not for [yours] only but also for the whole world" (1 John 2:2). Jesus "Himself bore [your] sins in His own body on the cross, that [you] having died to sins, might live for righteousness" (1 Pet. 2:24).

Yes, you can defeat Satan and his corruptive ways in the righteousness of Jesus Christ. Corruption can be defeated in the power of Jesus' name and of His blood shed on the Cross for the redemption of mankind.

Satan, the force behind corruption, is unseen and treacherous. He continues to devour the inhabitants of the world by his corruptive schemes. You may seem to be "like a grasshopper in [your] own sight" (Num. 13:33). The fight against this formidable enemy may seem to be foolish, "but God had chosen the foolish things of the world to put to shame the wise, and God has chosen the weak things of the world to put to shame the things which are mighty; and the base things of the world and the things which are despised God has chosen, and the things which are not, to bring to nothing the things that are, that no flesh should glory in His presence" (1 Cor. 1:27–29).

The Lord said to Joshua as he led the conquest of the Promised Land, "Every place that the sole of your foot will tread upon I have given you" (Josh. 1:3). The actions done and being implemented by several organizations in cooperation with governments to combat corruption are already steps taken toward the conquest of corruption.

The secret to overcome and defeat corruption is aligning with God and living out His moral principles of righteousness. God is powerful. He is Almighty God. He is a loving God. He loves you, but He hates any form of unrighteousness because He is a righteous God. He "will fight for you, and you shall hold your peace" (Exod. 14:14). You can come against the power of corruption, and it will be defeated in the name of Jesus and the power of His blood. Only then will its stronghold be broken and you will win the fight against it.

God, in His infinite wisdom and grace, can work in you to enable you and to give to you the ability and strategy to come against Satan, the Corruptor, and his hordes of demons. He will give you what you need to break and defeat corruption in the workplace and in the marketplace and to extricate people being corrupted from the bondage of corruption by the evil one. "For though [you] walk in the flesh, [you] do not war according to the flesh. For the weapons of [your] warfare are not carnal but mighty in God for pulling down strongholds, casting down arguments and every high thing that exalts itself against the knowledge of God, bringing every thought into captivity to the obedience of Christ" (2 Cor. 10:3–5).

This brings us back to making the right decision as discussed in chapter one. There are two choices before you: one good, the other evil. One choice is to ride the tide of corruption; the other is to fight it with God-given wisdom and strategy. One choice is to submit to God and His moral will; the other is to submit to the corrupting influences of Satan and allow him to control your will and use you to obey and follow his corrupted ways.

The choice is yours to make, but you have to choose one. I hope you will make the right choice, as my friend did.

David, the Shepherd Boy,
Against Goliath, the Giant

King David was a small shepherd boy when God placed him in the place where his nation Israel was fighting with a formidable enemy against them. (See 1 Samuel 17.) Their enemy, the Philistines, had a champion among them, whose name was Goliath standing nine feet, nine inches tall. This giant was heavily equipped with armor: a bronze helmet, a heavy coat of mail, bronze protections for his legs, and a spear between his shoulders. He had an assistant carry his shield for him. So Goliath stood before the armies of Israel and defied them and asked for a man from among them to fight him. Saul, king of Israel, and his army were greatly discouraged for there was not a man among them who was a match against this giant.

But David, a small shepherd boy, saw Israel's enemy and took the cause to fight because Israel was helpless and humiliated. David stood up and faced the giant to fight against him in the name of God. The giant might have chuckled in disdain, thinking, "These Israelites must be funny, sending a ruddy boy against me, a champion! How dare this little boy come against me, a man of war from my youth? How can he fight me with his shepherd's staff and his slingshot and five small stones? Ha, ha, ha! He must be crazy!" Goliath must have chuckled and said,

"There is no need for my armor and my sword this time. I will just squeeze you with my hands, boy!"

Why was David so brave? Why did he not fear the formidable giant? Let's take a look at David's credentials as a shepherd boy:

- His strength.

- His dedication to his work and his concern for the helpless. When a lion or bear took a lamb out of the flock, he went after it and saved the lamb from its mouth.

- His courage. When the lion or bear came against him, he confronted and killed it.

- His faith in the God who had delivered him from being killed by the lions and bears that attacked his flock.

Goliath might have chuckled, but not for long. As Goliath drew toward David, he mocked and cursed him by his gods. But David said to him:

> "You come to me with a sword, with a spear, and with a javelin. But I come to you in the name of the Lord of hosts, the God of the armies of Israel, whom you have defied. This day the Lord will deliver you into my hand,

> and I will strike you and take your head of
> you. And this day I will give the carcasses of
> the camp of the Philistines to the birds of the
> air and the wild beasts of the earth, that all
> the earth may know that there is a God in
> Israel. Then all...shall know that the Lord
> does not save with sword and spear; for the
> battle is the Lord's, and He will give you into
> our hands."
>
> —1 Samuel 17:45–47

When Goliath drew near David, David ran toward him, took out a stone from his bag, and slung it on his slingshot. He struck the giant, and the stone sank in Goliath's forehead. The giant fell on his face to the ground: "So David prevailed over the Philistine with a sling and a stone, and struck the Philistine and killed him...and cut off his head" (vv. 48–51).

Think about this. You may feel inadequate. People may look down upon you and doubt your ability. You may even doubt your own ability, but with God's help, He can do the impossible through you. You are a special creation of God. He made you for His special purpose—for good! You are fearfully and wonderfully made (Ps. 139:14). He loves you and wants to give you His best.

Would you like to be a David? David's secret in slaying the giant was his faith in God. You can be a David too! You can slay the social giant in your midst called by the name of Corruption. Being like David and having his secret is easy. You can talk to God in prayer as if He is right in front of you by praying this simple prayer:

Dear God, I desire to be like David. As You used him to slay Goliath, the giant that oppressed his people, use me in Your power and for Your glory to fight against the giant of corruption. Do this, so that You may set people free from oppression and poverty. I know that I have no power, no ability, no wisdom, and no strength to come against the power of the Corruptor, Satan, and to break his works of corruption. The only strength I have is in You and through Your own power and strength. Forgive me for thinking I can do everything I want to do in my life without You. Fill me with Your life and with Your presence, dear God. Help me to live my life in Jesus. I declare that You in me and I in You can overcome the power of the Corruptor because Your Son Jesus overcame him on the Cross. Jesus rose from the dead in Your resurrection power. I acknowledge Jesus' blood shed for me gives me the power to overcome corruption. Thank You, Jesus. Amen.

Chapter 15

THE REAL ISSUE

WHEN ADAM SINNED, his godly image was corrupted and he fell out of the grace of God. Adam's descendants—which is you and all the rest of mankind—inherited Adam's sinful human nature and were separated from the grace of the holy God. By disobeying God's command not to eat of the fruit of the forbidden tree, Adam allowed for himself and acquired for his descendants, the entire human race, the ability to know between good and evil, but also the capacity to do good or evil as each person decides for himself to do. We have the power to receive the grace of God by submitting to God's commands or to receive death for sins committed in obedience to the wiles of the devil.

Corruption perverts established rules or laws or moral

conduct, and lawlessness is sin (1 John 3:4). He who works corruption, "who sins is of the devil, for the devil has sinned from the beginning. For this purpose the Son of God was manifested, that He might destroy the works of the devil" (v. 8). God sent His Son, Jesus, who is perfect God, the second person of the Trinity, in the person of the Son of Man" to live in the flesh with men on the earth for thirty-three years, and He did so without committing any sin. God made Jesus "who knew no sin to be sin for us, that we might become the righteousness of God in Him" (2 Cor. 5:21).

While on the earth, Jesus manifested that He was sent of the Father by the many miracles that He did. He fed five thousand men by multiplying five loaves of bread and two fish and still leaving twelve basketfuls of leftovers (Matt. 14:15–21; Luke 9:12–17; John 6:14; Mark 6:32–44). He did the same miracle again by feeding four thousand men by multiplying seven loaves and a few little fish, and the fragments gathered after everyone had eaten were seven large basketfuls (Mark 8:1–9).

Aren't we also hungry, physically and spiritually, for God's miracles of righteous deliverance in these uncertain and turbulent times?

At the wedding feast in Cana, when the wine had run out, Jesus turned plain water into sweet wine (John 2:1–10). After a night of fruitless fishing, He told His disciples where to cast the net, and when they obeyed Him, they caught a great number of fish. Their net was breaking, and two boats were sinking when filled with the catch, it was so great (Luke 5:4–7). He healed the sick of various diseases, torments, and afflictions, and cast out demons too (Matt. 4:24). "The blind saw and the lame walked; the lepers were cleansed and the deaf heard; the dead were raised up and the poor had the gospel preached to them" (Matt. 11:5). The storm, the winds, and the waves obeyed His command" (Mark 4:39; Matt. 8:26).

Jesus told people to repent of their sins that corrupt them so they would not perish. And He said to them, "Thus it is written, and thus it was necessary for the Christ to suffer and to rise from the dead the third day, and that repentance and remission of sins should be preached in His name to all nations, beginning at Jerusalem" (Luke 24:46–47).

Jesus said, "Most assuredly, I say to you, he who believes in Me has everlasting life. I am the bread of life. I am the living bread which came down from heaven. If anyone eats of this bread, he will live forever; and the bread that I shall give is My flesh, which I shall give for the life of the world.... The words that I speak to you are spirit, and they are life" (John 6:47–48, 51, 63).

Jesus came to offer His own body, and by that one offering He has perfected forever "those who are being sanctified" (Heb. 9:27–28). Jesus took upon His own body the blows, the stripes, the beatings, the scourging, the ridicule, the mocking, and the unkind words and accusations that you and I deserved for our iniquities and our wickedness. He wore the crown of thorns on His head and caught the arrows the devil continues to aim at our minds to torture and to tempt us. Our corrupt works were nailed in the palms of His hands and His feet.

Jesus tooked the punishment we deserved on His own body on the cross, and no words of condemnation was even uttered by Him. And yet, with such words of great love, He prayed, "Father, forgive them, for they do not know what they do" (Luke 23:34). He had forgiven us for the sins we have done. He submitted Himself to all the punishment due for us "as a lamb to the slaughter, and as a sheep before its shearers is silent, so He opened not His mouth" (Isa. 53:7). We were there with the Roman soldiers who crucified Him. We were there with the Pharisees and the crowd who condemned Him to death.

And after completely offering His sinless body and taking all the punishment that we deserved, Jesus said, "It is finished" (John 19:30). He perfected the sacrifice that was needed to save us from being doomed to corruption unto eternal death. Jesus finished, completed, and perfected the offering of His body as an eternal sacrifice for you: "You were not redeemed with corruptible things, like silver or gold, from your aimless conduct...but with the precious blood of Christ" (1 Pet. 1:18–19). You were saved completely from the hand of the enemy who is warring against God for your soul. Satan succeeded in tweaking Adam's godly image by imputing his nature of corruption into Adam and his descendants. He succeeded in snatching Adam's dominion authority over the earth. But through the sacrifice of Jesus at the Cross, God made it possible for you and me to come back to God and obtain that precious relationship that Adam lost for himself and for us when he sinned, because, "if you sin, you have an Advocate with the Father, Jesus Christ the righteous. And He Himself is the propitiation for [your] sins, and not for [yours] only but also for the whole world" (1 John 2:1–2). God has made available for you the dominion authority over the earth which was snatched by the devil from Adam and his descendants. It is only then that you can defeat corruption and its author, Satan, in the power and the strength of Jesus and the reality of His finished sacrifice at the cross of Calvary.

In Christ, you can claim back the dominion authority over the earth that Adam lost to the devil. You can pray to God and call Him your Father and ask, "Your kingdom come, Your will be done on earth as it is in heaven" (Matt. 6:10). The kingdom of God is not living your life on the earth just by eating and drinking, but by living in the righteousness of Christ and the peace and joy of the Holy Spirit (Rom. 14:17). If you place your trust in Jesus Christ and believe in the efficacy and finality of His sacrifice on the Cross for your salvation, you can live the rest of your life here on the earth enjoying the authority over the things of the world: "For whatever is born of God overcomes the world. And this is the victory that has overcome the world—our faith" (1 John 5:4).

God's plan continues through all generations and will surely come to pass. Jesus had done all that was needed by God to bring into fullness His good plan and future for you. He did it completely and perfectly through the offering of His body for your sanctification. The blood of Jesus was shed for the remission of your sins. It is final. It is perfect. You can add nothing to what Jesus did for you to save you from the corruption of sin.

Jesus was buried in an empty tomb. But after three days, as He had said to His disciples, He was raised up from the dead in great resurrection power. His disciples and many others saw Him for forty days, and He spoke of things concerning the kingdom of God.

Before being taken up into heaven, Jesus said to His disciples, "You shall receive power when the Holy Spirit has come upon you; and you shall be witnesses to Me in Jerusalem, and in all Judea and Samaria, and to the end of the earth" (Acts 1:8). And then He was taken up in the clouds up to heaven.

And while His disciples watched steadfastly toward heaven, men in white apparel stood by them and said, "Men of Galilee, why do you stand gazing up into heaven? This same Jesus who was taken up from you into heaven, will so come in like manner as you saw Him go into heaven" (vv. 9–11).

Jesus died for you. He rose from the dead after three days. He is alive, seated at the right hand of the Father on high. He is praying for you to overcome corruption. He is coming again for you who overcome the power of corruption!

As the Holy Spirit came down to the disciples on Pentecost, the Father will send the Holy Spirit to you and to all who will believe in Jesus' finished work of redemption on the cross. The Helper will teach you all things and bring to remembrance all things Jesus had said. He is the guarantee of your inheritance until the day of your redemption (John 14:26; Eph. 1:14). The Holy Spirit continues to "convict the world of sin, and of righteousness, and of judgment: of sin because of the world's unbelief in [Jesus]; of righteousness because [Jesus went to His] Father and you see [Him] no more; and of judgment because the ruler of this world [Satan] is judged" (John 16:8–11).

God says to you, "I, even I, am He who blots out your transgression for My own sake; and I will not remember your sins. Put Me in remembrance; let us contend together; state your case, that you may be acquitted" (Isa. 43:25–26).

This is the real issue!

"The whole world lies under the sway of the wicked one" (1 John 5:19), Satan, who keeps on working his plan of conquering men through Corruption. But "the Son of

God has come and has given us an understanding, that
we may know Him who is true...this is the true God and
eternal life" (1 John 5:20). God will give you this understanding in the knowledge of Him if you will ask Jesus to
come into your heart and rule in your life.

The apostle Paul in his letter to the Ephesians prayed
for the church at Ephesus, and it is the same prayer I pray
for all who read this book:

> *That the God of our Lord Jesus Christ, the
> Father of glory, may give to you the Spirit
> of wisdom and revelation in the knowledge
> of Him, the eyes of your understanding being
> enlightened; that you may know what is the
> hope of His calling, what are the riches of the
> glory of His inheritance in the saints, and
> what is the exceeding greatness of His power
> toward [you] who believe, according to the
> working of His mighty power which He
> worked in Christ when He raised Him from
> the dead and seated Him at His right hand
> in the heavenly places, far above all princi-
> pality and power and might and dominion,
> and every name that is named, not only in
> this age but also in that which is to come.
> Amen (Eph. 1:17–21).*

NOTES

Chapter 1
Life's Two Choices

1. NOAA Ocean Service Education, "Currents," http://oceanservice
.noaa.gov/education/kits/currents/03coastal3.html (accessed on February
26, 2011).

2. Ibid.

Chapter 3
What Is Corruption?

1. INTERPOL, "INTERPOL Group of Experts on Corruption
(IGEC)," http://www.interpol.int/Public/Corruption/IGEC/Default.
asp" (accessed February 27, 2011).

2. Transparency International: http://www.transparency.org/; the
2010 Corruption Perceptions Index report: http://www.transparency.
org/policy_research/surveys_indices/cpi/2010/results (accessed March 5,
2011).

3. Fact sheet, CIA World Fact Book: https://www.cia.gov/library/
publications/the-world-factbook/rankorder/2010rank.html (accessed
March 5, 2011).

4. Jennifer Horton, "How Octopuses Work," How Stuff Works,
http://animals.howstuffworks.com/marine-life/octopus.htm (accessed
February 27, 2011).

5. Ibid.

6. Hillary Mayell, "Octopus Arms May Point Way to New Robot
Designs," National Geographic News, http://news.nationalgeographic.
com/news/2005/02/0209_050209_octopus.html (accessed February 27,
2011).

7. Footnote for Isaiah 14:12–14, *New Scofield Study Bible* (Nashville, TN: Thomas Nelson, 1989).

8. *The Real Truth Magazine*, "Corruption: A Worldwide Scourge Soon to End," June 10, 2007, http://www.realtruth.org/articles/070601 -003-cawsste.html (accessed August 29, 2010).

CHAPTER 5
WAYS CORRUPTION WORKS

1. Wikipedia.com, "Bribery," http://en.wikipedia.org/wiki/Bribery (accessed October 9, 2010).

2. *Merriam-Webster's Dictionary*, s.v. "bribery."

3. Ibid., s.v. "bribe."

4. Wikipedia.com, "Bribery," http://en.wikipedia.org/wiki/Bribery (accessed February 27, 2011).

5. Ibid.

6. Rick Olivares, "Corruption: An Inconvenient Truth, Part 1," PoliticalArena.com, http://ph.politicalarena.com/noynoy-aquino/blogs/ corruption-an-inconvenient-truth-part-1 (accessed August 29, 2010).

7. *Merriam-Webster's Dictionary*, s.v. "bureaucracy."

8. HistoryofRock.com, "Payola," http://www.history-of-rock.com/ payola.htm (accessed September 13, 2010).

9. Ibid.

10. Wikipedia.com, "Extortion," http://en.wikipedia.org/wiki/ Extortion (accessed February 28, 2011).

11. Ibid.

12. *Merriam-Webster's Dictionary*, s.v. "nepotism."

13. AskDefine.com, "Cronyism," http://cronyism.askdefine.com/ (accessed February 28, 2011).

14. Ibid.

15. Randy David, "No Place for Buddies," October 13, 2010, *Philippine Daily Inquirer*, as posted on Inquirer.net, http://opinion.

inquirer.net/inquireropinion/columns/view/20101013-297606/No-place-for-buddies (accessed January 26, 2011).

16. Ibid.

17. U.S. Securities and Exchange Commission, "Insider Trading," http://www.sec.gov/answers/insider.htm (accessed August 15, 2010).

18. Ibid.

19. Yahoo News Canada, "Employee Charged with Selling Secrets: WSJ," http://ca.news.finance.yahoo.com/s/150821emplyee-charged -selling-secrets-wsj.html (accessed August 15, 2010).

20. Canadian Press, "Tax Agency Probes Restaurants that Hide Cash Sales," as posted on CTV News, http://www.ctv.ca/CTVNews/ Canada/20091109/phantom_tax_091109/ (accessed February 28, 2011).

CHAPTER 6
OTHER WAYS OF CORRUPTION

1. Encyclopedia Britannica, "Roe v. Wade," http://www.britannica .com/EBchecked/topic/506705/Roe-v-Wade (accessed October 31, 2010).

2. Karen Blanks Adams, *Life in the Matrix* (Lake Mary, FL: Creation House, 2010).

3. Affidavit of Norma McCorvey, formerly known as Jane Roe, Plaintiff, civil Action No. 3-3690-B and No. 3-3601-C, http://www .thejusticefoundation.org/images/64456/NormaMcCorveyAffidavit.pdf (accessed October 31, 2010).

4. Ibid.

5. Ibid, emphasis added.

6. United States Court of Appeals, Fifth Circuit Division, *McCorvey v. Hill*, No.03-10711, September 14, 2004, http://caselaw.findlaw.com/ us-5th-circuit/1344628.html (accessed October 31, 2010).

7. Ibid., emphasis added.

8. Terry Law and Jim Gilbert, *The Hope Habit: Finding God's Goodness When Life Is Hard* (Lake Mary, FL: Charisma House, 2010), 142.

9. Ibid., 145.

10. Ibid., 71.

11. John F. Burns, "Cricket Scandal Rocks Pakistan," August 29, 2010, *New York Times*, http://www.nytimes.com/2010/08/30/world/europe/30cricket.html?_r=1&hpw (accessed February 28, 2011).

CHAPTER 9
HOW CORRUPTION CONTROLS THE WORLD

1. Chuck Pierce and Rebecca Wagner Systema, *Possessing Your Inheritance: Moving Forward in God's Covenant Plan for Your Life* (Ventura, CA: Regal Books, 1999), 179.

CHAPTER 11
THE EFFECTS OF CORRUPTION

1. Associated Press, "UK Man Completes 4,200-Mile Amazon Trek on Foot," CBSNews.com, August 9, 2010, http://www.cbsnews.com/stories/2010/08/09/world/main6756306.shtml (accessed February 28, 2011).

CHAPTER 13
MITIGATING CORRUPTION

1. UNCAC, convention: http://www.unodc.org/unodc/en/treaties/CAC/index.html (accessed March 3, 2011).

2. UNCAC, pulications: http://www.unodc.org/documents/treaties/UNCAC/publications/convention/08-50026_E.pdf (accessed March 18, 2011).

3. OECD.org, "About the Organisation for Economic Co-operation and Development (OECD)," http://www.oecd.org/pages/0,3417,en_36734052_36734103_1_1_1_1_1,00.html (accessed February 28, 2011).

4. OECD.org, "OECD Convention on Combating Bribery of Foreign Public Officials in International Business Transactions," http://www

.oecd.org/document/21/0,3746,en_2649_37447_2017813_1_1_1_37447,00
.html (accessed February 28, 2011).

5. Millennium Challenge Corporation, "About MCC," http://www
.mcc.gov/pages/about (accessed February 28, 2011).

6. Millennium Challenge Corporation, "Fighting Corruption,"
https://www.mcc.gov/pages/activities/activity/fighting-corruption
(accessed February 28, 2011).

7. The World Bank, "About Us," http://web.worldbank.org/
WBSITE/EXTERNAL/EXTABOUTUS/0,,pagePK:50004410~piPK:
36602~theSitePK:29708,00.html (accessed February 28, 2011).

8. The World Bank, "Overview of Anticorruption," http://
web.worldbank.org/WBSITE/EXTERNAL/TOPICS/
EXTPUBLICSECTORANDGOVERNANCE/EXTANTICORRU
PTION/0,,contentMDK:21540659~menuPK:384461~pagePK:148956~piP
K:216618~theSitePK:384455,00.html (accessed February 28, 2011).

9. GOPAC: http://www.gopacnetwork.org (accessed March 3, 2011).

10. Transparency International: http://www.transparency.org
(accessed March 3, 2011).

11. The World Economic Forum, http://www.transparency.org
(accessed February 28, 2011).

12. Cielito Habito, "No Free Lunch: Regaining the People's Trust,"
Philippine Daily Inquirer, June 29, 2010, as posted on Inquirer.net, http://
services.inquirer.net/print/print.php?article_id=2010629-278133 (accessed
October 23, 2010).

ABOUT
THE AUTHOR

Angelita Marasigan gained more than thirty years experience in project development and contracts administration in her job as a civil engineer in the public and private sector. She has long retired from this job and now lives with her family in Canada.

CONTACT
THE AUTHOR

By e-mail:
drealissue@rogers.com

www.ingramcontent.com/pod-product-compliance
Lightning Source LLC
LaVergne TN
LVHW051054080426
835508LV00019B/1863